One Chance
A Memoir

PAUL POTTS

WEINSTEIN
BOOKS

Printed and bound by CPI Group (UK) Ltd, Croydon, CR0 4YY.

Cataloging-in-Publication data for this book is available
from the Library of Congress.
ISBN: 978-1-60286-228-9 (print)
ISBN: 978-1-60286-229-6 (e-book)
ISBN: 978-1-60286-238-8 (United Kingdom print)
ISBN: 978-1-60286-239-5 (United Kingdom e-book)

Published by Weinstein Books
A member of the Perseus Books Group
www.weinsteinbooks.com

Weinstein Books are available at special discounts for bulk purchases
in the U.S. by corporations, institutions and other organizations.
For more information, please contact the Special Markets Department at the
Perseus Books Group, 2300 Chestnut Street, Suite 200, Philadelphia, PA 19103,
call (800) 810-4145, ext. 5000, or e-mail special.markets@perseusbooks.com.

Editorial production by *Marra*thon Production Services.
www.marrathon.net

Book design by Ellen E Rosenblatt/SD Designs, LLC.
Set in 11.5 point Bauer Bodoni

First edition

10 9 8 7 6 5 4 3 2 1

Oldham
Council

One Chance

I'd like to dedicate this book to Julz,
my long-suffering wife, without whom I'd be lost.

FOREWORD

By Simon Cowell

I HAVE SAT THROUGH a lot of auditions through the last decade, some good and a lot not so good! But there are a few auditions I will always remember for special reasons, and one of those is Paul Potts's.

It was the first season on *Britain's Got Talent*, back in 2007. The auditions weren't going great and I was genuinely worried whether we were going to find a star. We arrived in Cardiff and the day was not going very well but I remember a shy man in a funny suit walking onto the stage. I looked over to Piers, Piers rolled his eyes as Paul quietly told us he was an opera singer, then I rolled my eyes! Then he started to sing. I will never forget that moment—the atmosphere in the theatre changed in an instant, he literally raised the roof, and I knew our show was safe.

Over time I got to know Paul as a person and I got to know his other qualities. Paul has real courage; he overcame the bullying of his childhood as well as the many other obstacles life had thrown his way. Paul also has such dedication; he is someone who was always going to work hard to achieve his dream of a singing career.

Paul's road to success reads like a film script, and now it has been turned into a movie. This couldn't happen to a nicer guy; he is genuinely one of the warmest, friendliest guys I have had the pleasure of working with. I am delighted and proud that we were able to give him that original chance, but everything else has been down to him.

PROLOGUE

What a Difference a Day Makes

I WILL NEVER FORGET that fateful day. That dull, wet Saturday morning on St. Patrick's Day in 2007 when I arrived at the Millennium Centre in Cardiff to audition for *Britain's Got Talent.*

My father was panicking that my wife, Julz, and I would be late. The audition was the same day as a Wales-England rugby match, and having set off from our home in Port Talbot, we hit the traffic just outside Llantrisant, about fourteen miles from Cardiff. My phone began vibrating in my pocket. I looked at the screen, and it was Dad, who was already at the venue.

"The people are already going in!" he said, with an audible scowl.

"Stop worrying," I said. "They're probably contestants from an earlier round of auditions."

But however much I tried to reassure him, I couldn't calm his nerves. He kept on calling me as we made our way up the M4.

I had been strangely subdued on the drive up, but once I

reached the concert hall, all that changed. We still had some time to wait before I was sent to the holding area, and having no clue what time I would be going on, I was beginning to get quite nervous. I picked up my number from the check-in area—31829, which I stuck sideways on my jacket—and made my way up the stairs to the auditorium. The holding area was a bar behind the upper circle, and it was a very busy room, with hundreds of people scrambling round for seats and plenty of film crews to capture every moment of rehearsal on tape. Through the walls we could hear the proceedings of the previous group: the noise of the audience rippled through, as did the sound of the dreaded buzzer. That silenced the crowd in the holding room immediately. It was something none of us wanted to hear when it was our turn to be on stage.

I'd read advice online from previous contestants, who suggested you should make as much noise as possible, dress wildly, and practise hard to make sure you ended up on film. In fact, to do just about anything to stand out from the crowd. But that was the last thing I wanted to do. While others were rehearsing loudly to catch the attention of the cameras, I attempted to fade into the background like a wallflower.

I wasn't here to make a career out of what I was about to do. Instead, I was here to finish a journey that had started at the age of six. Singing was something I loved doing, but I could see no future in it.

"Hi there, can I ask what you're here to do?"

My thoughts were interrupted by a guy in a pale-blue fleece coat from the production team and his colleague holding a TV camera. It's strange that a previously coherent person can become a jabbering wreck when facing a large piece of electronics placed on someone's shoulder. It took me some time to pluck up the courage to even say a very weak "hello." It was right about then that I started to have second thoughts about being there.

I didn't really know what to say, and ended up blurting out the first thing that came into my head.

"I'm here to sing opera," I told the guy. "It's something I feel I was born to do."

"That's great," the guy replied. "How about singing something for us here and now, a cappella?"

I responded with a very nervous look towards Julz, and a very fast shake of the head. "I don't want to do that," I said.

I wanted to go back to being the wallflower. I felt I wasn't the kind of person who should be in front of people, in full view. I felt fat and slightly scruffy. The suit I was wearing was all I could afford, and for some reason I had insisted on buying one that was too small in the chest but at the same time too long in the arms. The last thing I wanted to do was draw further attention to the fact that I didn't really belong here. Reluctantly, the member of the production crew accepted my refusal to sing. He finished our quick chat and moved on to another person.

I tried and failed to find out when I would be on stage. This was disconcerting, as I always like to be well prepared so as to perform at my best. But now I was faced with no warm-up area, no sound check, and no timetable. I did my best to try to find somewhere private enough to warm up, and ended up in the gents' toilets. Even there, I didn't want to sing in front of anyone. The moment I heard footsteps approaching, I pushed the lever of the tap as if to wash my hands. There appeared to be no way of warming up at all. After a while, I just gave up and returned to my seat next to Julz.

A different member of the production approached me, this time from ITV2, ITV's second channel. He was filming for the spin-off show to *Britain's Got Talent*: *Britain's Got More Talent*. This guy was very relaxed and funny, and asked me to go with him. I was a little reluctant, but Julz persuaded me.

"Go on, Paul," she whispered. "Just for once do as you're told!"

Julz and I share a very healthy sense of humour, in spite of having gone through some pretty difficult times. So I followed her command and walked out with the crew. Initially they wanted me to sing in the corridor surrounded by lots of people. But when they noticed my reticence, they changed tack and suggested we go outside.

Luckily the rain had stopped and there weren't too many people around. With the wind blowing, I launched into the last full phrase of "Nessun Dorma," the aria made famous by the great Luciano Pavarotti, and which was used as the theme for the 1990 World Cup:

Dilegua, o notte! Tramontate, stelle! Tramontate, stelle!
All'alba vincerò! Vincerò! Vince-e-erò!

I just about felt okay doing it. However, while I was filming outside with the *Britain's Got More Talent* crew, the three *Britain's Got Talent* judges—Simon Cowell, Amanda Holden, and Piers Morgan—were giving a briefing to all the other contestants about what was about to happen. Not only had I missed that, but my name had been called as one of the first contestants to go on. I got upstairs with the crew and there was Dad again, panicking about the fact that my name had been called. There wasn't a moment to spare—it was time to go.

Backstage, I felt like Daniel about to be thrown into the lion's den. I hadn't warmed up properly, and now I was being unexpectedly thrust straight in, not knowing what was going to happen. What had started as a day out—and an opportunity to perform at Wales's latest, and arguably greatest, concert hall— was turning into the worst kind of nightmare.

I wasn't built for risks. I just didn't take them. I had never even bet on the Grand National or Derby, and now I was about to perform in front of two thousand people, including one of the people in the music business I respected most: Simon Cowell. I would have been nervous enough if I'd just come fresh from a run as principal tenor with a local company. But I was about to go on stage, having barely sung a note in public for nearly four years.

The last major singing I had done was in the role of Chevalier des Grieux in Puccini's *Manon Lescaut* for Southgate Opera, an amateur company based in North London. For that kind of performance, I was playing a role: I was des Grieux, or Radames, or whatever part I was playing. I could hide behind the costume of the General of the Imperial Guard of Egypt, fighting for the love of Aida and Egypt at the same time. Now I was about to sing as myself, and I felt naked. I was going on as Paul Potts, and soon I would learn whether I was worthy of a place on stage.

I still didn't know whether I would have to sing a cappella, as I had witnessed on other talent shows like *The X Factor* and

American Idol. I had watched the early rounds of those shows and dreaded being one of the performers viewers laughed at. I had brought my backing-track disc in the hope that I would be able to use it, but was prepared for the worst—that I might have to sing with no music to accompany me.

A member of the stage crew asked me if I was okay.

"I'd feel much better if I could use my backing track," I explained.

"Do you have it with you?" he asked.

I pulled it out of my jacket pocket and said, "It's track number eight. Thank you very much." I was hugely relieved, because performing a cappella is one of the things that frightens me most.

The crew member took my CD and told me I'd be next on after a dancer and her partner. I watched from the side as they went on stage and did their audition. The lady danced with a pashmina scarf while the man performed birdsong by whistle. It didn't go down well.

"Off! Off! Off!" the crowd screamed, baying for blood.

I was petrified. The prospect of going out in front of a crowd shouting for me to leave was something that frightened the living daylights out of me. What have I let myself in for? I asked myself. But there was no time to think about that, as the couple was dismissed from the stage and I was told that my time had come.

I walked out. "Shuffled out," as Simon would later put it. I seriously considered just running out the other side. Would that have been any sillier than performing? My mind was still debating that when Amanda spoke.

"What are you here for today, Paul?"

My legs were shaking as I answered, "To sing opera."

"Ready when you are," Simon said, motioning for me to start.

I gave a loud sigh. This was it: I had no choice now but to stay and sing. I nodded towards the wings for the crew member to press play on my backing track.

The music began. I tried to settle myself, but my legs were like jelly. I looked directly at Simon, Piers, and Amanda, hoping against hope they would like my performance. Because of the dazzling stage lights I couldn't really see them very clearly, which only added to my nerves. I decided to try and ignore the judges completely and treat it as a performance rather than an audition. As I began singing the first few phrases, I couldn't help thinking this might be the last time I would ever perform. I found myself putting more emotion into the aria. When I got to the famous musical phrase that is repeated later as *"Dilegua, o notte"* in "Nessun Dorma" for the first time, I could hear the audience reacting to my performance with applause and cheers. I ignored the sound and did my best to stay focused and put everything into what I genuinely believed was going to be my swan song.

The music reached the section in the aria where the female chorus comes in, and I knew the big climax was on its way. I threw body and soul into it, determined to really nail the high B natural that comes at the end. Generally for me, the high B is the easier of the last two notes to sing. The vowel shape is one that I felt on previous practise to be more friendly than the more closed "rawh" of the last high A. On reaching the B, however, I was horrified. I had put so much into it that I had ended up with too much tension in my voice. The note didn't come out the way I would have liked.

PROLOGUE

I finished my audition bitterly disappointed. I felt that my very last performance had been an underachievement. This was despite the fact that the audience were now on their feet. It was apparent that they had enjoyed what they heard, but I felt it was inevitable that the judges would know I had messed it up. I had let myself down at the most crucial part of the aria, and I didn't particularly want to hear what Simon had to say. He was bound to hate it because I had messed up the note that everyone remembers. I waited for his response, but the one I got was not the one I was anticipating.

"So you work in Carphone Warehouse, and you did that. I wasn't expecting that at all. This was a complete breath of fresh air. I thought you were absolutely fantastic."

He did have reservations, though. He told me that I had shuffled on stage like I was apologising for being there, I looked terrible. And the suit I was wearing was too big for me. (I neglected to mention to him that although the sleeves were indeed too long, I had no hope of actually doing up the buttons on the jacket!)

"I don't care if you come on naked if you sing like that!" interrupted Piers. "You have an incredible voice." And to my huge surprise, he added, "If you keep singing like that, you're going to be one of the favourites to win the whole competition."

Next it was Amanda's turn. "I think . . . that we've got a case of a little lump of coal here that is going to turn into a diamond."

It was difficult to take in what I was hearing. I wasn't expecting anything positive to come out of this, yet they liked my voice. Before I had a chance to get my head round the compliments, it was time for the judges to vote.

"Okay," Simon said. "Moment of truth, young man." He looked across to his fellow judges.

"Absolutely yes," said Piers.

"Amanda?" asked Simon.

"Yes." Amanda nodded.

"Paul"—Simon looked at me with a smile—"you are through to the next round."

As the audience cheered, I was in complete shock. I had arrived at the audition expecting this performance to be my last, so getting through to the next stage was a huge surprise for me. Instead of my singing career coming to a close, I was about to embark on a musical journey that would change my life forever.

PART ONE

Beginnings

CHAPTER ONE

Childhood

"RACE YOU!"

It was a warm, sunny summer's day in my home town of Bristol, and my mother had taken my older brother, John, and me to Vassals Park for a treat. Vassals Park, or Oldbury Court Estate, was one of the best green spaces in the city. It had history, being old enough to be mentioned in the Domesday Book, but as a young boy I didn't care about any of that. I just wanted to run about and have fun.

As soon as we arrived, John and I ran over to the play area. There were swings, a sand pit, and an early form of treadmill: two wooden drums on a spindle with a set of metal pipes alongside.

"Bet you can't go as fast as me," John boasted as we took turns. We carried on running while Mum sat on a bench watching us, getting on with her knitting. We played on that treadmill for ages (perhaps that's why both John and I became interested in running later on) before Mum decided it was time to go.

"Does anyone fancy an ice cream?" she asked, knowing this was the best way to get us to move.

This was turning out to be a great afternoon. We bought our ice creams from the resident van and ate them hungrily as we walked the long way home. We rarely went back the same way we got to the park—a habit I still follow. The three of us would walk through the whole of Oldbury Court Estate, pausing from time to time to play in the River Frome. We reached Snuff Mills and had a look at the old mill wheel. There was a café there, where sometimes we'd get our ice creams. The owners knew us and would sometimes give us a few extra sweets on top. The walk ensured that we got to experience the river; the feel of the waterfall always made us feel cool, and the force of it was awe inspiring.

We walked on, climbing back up Blackberry Hill, which felt enormous when you had short legs. By now the heat was getting to me, and I was gasping for thirst.

"Can we stop at the shop and get something to drink?" I asked.

Mum shook her head. "No, Paul, we've got pop back at home."

The thought of pop to drink back at the house briefly got John and me excited.

"Council pop," Mum corrected.

I sighed in disappointment. "Council pop" was of course tap water.

I was born and grew up in Bristol, and have always felt lucky to have done so. Bristol is a fantastic city. It has always been a vibrant and exciting place to live, and boasts its own musical and cultural identity. With Wales just across the Severn Bridge, the Forest of Dean to the north, and the holiday resorts of Devon and Cornwall a short drive to the south, it is perfectly situated to enjoy some of Britain's most beautiful countryside. As with many large British cities in the 1970s and 1980s, it had its share of problems, but that never took away from what made it a special place.

My family lived in the Fishponds area of Bristol. We lived in a Victorian terraced house, which wasn't small but not exactly big, either, for a large family like ours. I am the second oldest of four children: John is the oldest, then it's me and the twins, Tony and Jane. I could describe us as living from hand to mouth, and perhaps by today's standards we were, but we had the basics.

Were we poor? It depends what you measure it against. We were fed, watered, and clothed, and in reality there isn't much you can ask for apart from that. Our clothes were rarely brand new, unless a school uniform grant was provided for their purchase. When we had a television, it was rented from Radio Rentals.

Dad did many different jobs, all of them manual labour, which paid only just about enough. Mum did some work from home, knitting jumpers and gloves to order. Every little bit helps, as the saying goes.

Mum came from a coal-mining community in South Wales called Abertillery. Strangely enough, Julz's dad lived a few streets behind her, and Julz's grandfather and my maternal grandfather both worked in the same pit together. We always enjoyed going to see Nanny Beat (short for Beatrice) and Grandcha, as we called our grandfather. Grandcha could be a little mischievous sometimes: he once offered my older brother a pound if he would cut the grass—a lot of money for a small boy back then. When John said yes, he handed him a very rusty pair of shears for him to work with. It was just as well that John was resourceful from an early age.

We saw signs for the M4 motorway to South Wales very frequently as we walked round Bristol, and longed for our next trip there. It wasn't that our grandparents spoiled us with material things; it was more because they, and my grandcha in particular, doted on their grandchildren. Grandcha once made the trip to Bristol by himself without telling Nanny Beat where he was going, just so he could see us. That involved quite a difficult journey by bus, including several changes along the way. He got into trouble with Nanny because he left without telling her where he was going, but he didn't care. He just wanted to see his grandchildren.

As with my grandparents, there was a definite power balance in our own house, but in this case the power was on the man's side. Mum was, and has always been, the mild-mannered, quiet, hard-working sort of person who got on with her life with few complaints. Dad, by contrast, was the disciplinarian. On the whole, we were all well behaved, but there were times when we wouldn't listen and we'd hear the immortal words, "Wait 'til your father gets home!" That usually got the desired effect.

As is often the case, my siblings and I were quite different from each other. My older brother was born just over a year before me, while Tony and Jane, the twins, were born just under two years later. These differences became apparent as we got older. John had the gift of the gab. He always seemed to know what to say and what to do. When he got to school, he knew exactly how to deal with the strong characters on the playground. I, by contrast, didn't have a clue.

I wasn't a bad kid, but often I seemed to find myself getting into scrapes, especially when I was with Alex, one of my early friends. Alex was about the same age as me, with red hair and prominent freckles that really stood out in the summer. He was perhaps not the greatest of influences, and whenever we hung out, we'd egg each other on to see what we could get away with. More often than not, we ended up getting into mischief.

One day after school, Alex and I were playing at the bottom of the street. At the end of my road there was a filling station, and while we were messing about I noticed the safety shut-off switch at the back of the yard.

"Go on," I said. "I dare you to push the switch."

"Why?" Alex replied. "Are you too scared to push it yourself?"

We looked at each other to see who would be brave enough to push the switch to the pumps off position. After a delay, I took the plunge. Since I wasn't the tallest of children, I had to scramble up a wall to reach it. Even then it was harder than it looked, but I managed to push it up with both hands.

Somehow, I got away with it. No one had spotted us, and Alex and I went over to watch the bemused looks as drivers filling up their cars found their pumps had stopped operating. As the chaos unfolded, we chickened out and made a run for it before anyone saw us. Which was probably just as well: Mum worked in the garage as a part-time cleaner, and I'd have been in for it if I'd been caught.

On another occasion, Alex suggested we go by bike to St. Paul's, where his father worked. St. Paul's was a part of Bristol that in the early eighties was considered something of a no-go area, even in the daytime. A couple of years later, it made national headlines after rioting broke out. A bike trip to St. Paul's, therefore, was something of an adventure.

Alex had a Raleigh Chopper, which was the bike at the top of every boy's wish list back then. The Chopper looked like a small version of a Harley-Davidson, with the handlebars going out wide and a gear stick with three gears in front on the crossbar. It was to die for, particularly since I didn't have a bike.

"That's okay," Alex told me. "You can borrow my sister's bike."

His sister Caroline's bike was the height of trendiness at the time, but for *girls* rather than boys. Instead of being a Raleigh Chopper, it was a pale-blue Raleigh *Shopper*, complete with shopping basket on the front. I felt like an idiot, but the only other option was to run alongside Alex like a wimpy boxer out for a run with his ginger (red-haired) trainer. So without Caroline's knowing, I took her bike.

It was a three-mile journey from Fishponds to St. Paul's, through St. George and Easton. It was in Easton where things started to unravel. Alex, I quickly realized, was far more confident than I was on two wheels. I was struggling to keep up.

I was following Alex as he pedalled into the underpass above the M32, the motorway that links Bristol to the M4, the main road from London to South Wales. Today these underpasses have a marked cycle lane through them, but back then bikes were banned. That wasn't the only thing telling us we weren't meant to be there on two wheels: there was also a four-foot-high barrier made of metal tubing that went halfway across the path and another just behind it.

As an experienced cyclist, Alex didn't have a problem with the barriers. He dodged them both without even putting his feet on the ground or even slowing down very much. As a much less experienced cyclist, the sensible thing for me to do was to brake and walk my bike round. Instead of braking, however, I thought I would use the slope alongside the underpass tunnel to stop my momentum. I pointed the bike straight at the tunnel wall and pedalled ahead. *Wallop!* The bike hit the wall and I followed straight after with a loud crack.

The crack was my middle tooth, which I had chipped and exposed a nerve in. It was painful, and only became more so when I got back onto Caroline's bike and felt the wind whistle through it. To make matters worse, the Shopper hadn't come out well from the crash, either: The wheel had buckled in the fall, and I had to pedal even harder to get it to continue turning.

We made it to St. Paul's and then started to head back. All the time, the pain in my tooth was increasing. At least on the return journey I made sure to walk the by now complaining bicycle round the barriers. What followed was even more unpleasant. As we turned the corner into Alex's street, we could see a very displeased mother and daughter scowling at us. Alex was in trouble for not telling his mum where he was going, and we were both in the doghouse for taking Caroline's bike without asking, then bringing it back in such a mangled condition.

Because she didn't know where he was, Alex's mum had been

round to my house to see if he was there. I groaned. That meant my parents also knew I'd slipped off without permission. I trudged disconsolately home to a double whammy of punishment and a trip to the dentist.

The bike incident wasn't the only accident I was involved in growing up, and the next occasion was far more serious. It happened on a trip to Wales. I had been to a parade service for the Boys' Brigade (a Christian youth organisation) as I was being awarded a badge. After the service the plan was to drive to see Nanny Beat and Grandcha for lunch.

We didn't always have a car growing up, but at this time we had a Ford Escort van. It was brown, had a rear seat-bench and rear windows, and was a tight fit for the four of us children in the back. Tony and Jane, the youngest in the family, often sat in the very rear of the van as we travelled. This was an era when wearing seatbelts was not legally required. Seatbelts in the back were not even thought of at this point.

Dad hated wearing a seatbelt. He dreaded the upcoming law change that would make wearing them compulsory, saying that wearing it made him feel trapped. On this particular Sunday, however, my brother John had persuaded Dad to strap himself in. Dad had put it on to humour him, intending to remove it shortly thereafter. As it happened, Dad forgot he had it on, and he drove away from home with it still attached.

It took us some twenty-five minutes to get from our house to the motorway. We were all looking forward to our day trip to Nanny Beat's. These excursions were very special, and we'd stop at the Aust service station on the way back for a drink and a view across the Severn Bridge. This particular journey, however, was to prove memorable for all the wrong reasons.

It happened shortly after we pulled onto the motorway. We were travelling at about fifty miles per hour in the inside, or slow, lane, when there was a loud bang on the back of the van. We learned later that we had been hit by a driver who had fallen asleep at the wheel. His car was traveling at ninety-five miles per hour when it hit us. The van lurched as the other car hit us, and then everything went into a spin. Such was the impact that our van overturned five times into the central reservation (median strip), then rebounded back across the active lane before landing upside-down in the embankment.

It was while all this was happening that Mum risked her life trying to make sure we were okay. The overturning happened quickly, yet I can still see Mum climbing over the front seat, desperately checking on us even as the windscreen glass lacerated her legs. I was in the middle, and if Mum hadn't done that, the glass would have cut up my face.

We were lucky to be alive. The traffic police who attended the accident made it clear that our lives had been saved because we were travelling in a small passenger van. Ordinarily, with the way the accident occurred, we should have all been killed. Passenger vans weren't popular vehicles, and were cheaper to buy because they rarely had rear seats and windows. But they did have reinforced roofs, and that's what protected us when the van overturned.

Dad's life was saved by the fact that he was still wearing his seatbelt. Even so, he had severe bruising from being thrown against the steering wheel. Most of us just had cuts and bruises, though Jane wasn't so lucky. She was sitting by the right-hand window and had the worst of it. Her face was sliced open on the edge of her mouth and needed plastic surgery to put it right.

The accident was a huge shock to us all. Sitting in the back of the ambulance, I cried all the way to the hospital. It took us a long time to get the courage to return to the motorway after that. For a while we'd go to Nanny Beat's via a roundabout route of country lanes instead. To this day, I remember the site of the accident. On my trips back from Heathrow I think of it as we pass a sign that gives the mileage to Newport, Cardiff, and Swansea.

One other important memory from my early childhood is of a time when my father's disciplinarian side came head-to-head with Alex's mischief making. It was over an altercation with our next-door neighbour Mrs. Hunt. I was the one stuck in the middle, with painful repercussions that lingered long after the incident itself.

Mrs. Hunt had a son called Clive who once tripped John up against a wall, cutting his upper lip open and leaving a scar that my brother still has. Clive's response was to laugh at John's misfortune. Clive's mother was also someone we'd never got on well with. And if we were playing in our back garden and kicked a ball over the low wall, it was confiscated for good. In fact, Mrs. Hunt only returned these balls (all of them) many years later. We always found her a little stubborn and were too afraid to ask for the balls back.

On this occasion, Alex and I were playing at the bottom of the road as usual, when Mrs. Hunt passed us. It doesn't take much imagination to imagine what mischief children could get into with a name like Hunt. It wasn't something I would do, no matter how much I disliked my neighbours. Alex, however, found it extremely funny.

"Hey!" he shouted. "It's Mrs. C——."

As Alex shouted out the obscenity, he stood there laughing at the annoyance he had caused. The trouble was that Mrs. Hunt thought *I* had shouted at her. I watched in horror as she stormed up the street and knocked on our door. Before I knew it, there was my red-faced angry father shouting at me.

"Paul! Get in here right this instant!"

I looked round to Alex for support. But he, of course, had had the foresight to make himself scarce.

As I went inside, I wasn't sure who was more furious, my father or Mrs. Hunt.

"I want you to tell me exactly what you shouted at Mrs. Hunt," he said.

"I didn't shout anything," I replied. "It was Alex!"

"Don't hide behind your friend," Mrs. Hunt said. "I know it was you who shouted at me."

"It wasn't," I repeated. "Dad, it was Alex, not me!"

"Are you calling Mrs. Hunt a liar now?" Dad responded.

For a child to call an adult a liar was a serious accusation. But I stuck to the truth, and again insisted that it wasn't I who had shouted.

My father sent me out of the room and spoke with Mrs. Hunt alone. I was left cowering behind the living-room window, straining to hear what was being said. Mrs. Hunt was adamant that I had sworn at her, and wanted me to be disciplined.

"If you don't teach that boy how to behave, he'll become uncontrollable," she told my father. "It's unacceptable for a child to use language like that."

Ironically, I was in complete agreement with Mrs. Hunt over the obscenity; even to this day, that particular word is one I abhor. But neither this, nor the fact that I was telling the truth, was enough to save me: I got the strap of my father's belt no less than ten times. I was insistent to the end that I hadn't said it, being honest to the point of stupidity. The more I protested my innocence, the more strikes I got. I was upset, not so much about the beating, which at this time would have been seen as acceptable, since corporal punishment was still being carried out at school. I was upset more about not being believed, as I wasn't the sort to tell lies about this kind of incident.

In the end, my father believed me. I'm not sure exactly what made him change his mind, but the fact that I had taken a beating and stood by my word may have had something to do with it. He apologised and told Mrs. Hunt that I had been disciplined unnecessarily because of her insistence. Even then, she didn't back down. From then on, whenever she was walking on my side of the road, I crossed to the other side.

Early on in life, I learned the hard way that the only person I could rely on was myself. Alex, I realized, wasn't as dependable a friend as I'd thought he was. Rather than standing by my side, he buckled under pressure and left me to face my difficulties alone. When it came to school, as I was about to discover, I would have many such difficulties to deal with.

CHAPTER TWO

School

"COME ON, Paul," my mother said. "Are you sure you don't want to eat anything?"

It was breakfast time, but not like any I was used to. Today was my first day at Chester Park Infant School. My new school uniform felt scratchy and uncomfortable, and my stomach was tight with nerves.

"It's all right," I said. "I'm really not that hungry."

"Don't worry, love," my mother said, "it'll all be fine. And John will be there if you need help, won't you, John?"

I looked across at my older brother, happily wolfing down his breakfast without a care in the world. He had a natural confidence I wished I could share. Somehow, he had the knack of knowing what to say and what to do, and dealt easily with other people.

My own social skills were close to zero. To John, meeting people didn't appear to be a risk at all. To me, it felt like the most dangerous thing in the world. I didn't like uncertainty, and

I doubted myself the whole time. I preferred to hide in a corner and hope someone would approach me, saving me the risk of being rejected. I have always struggled in crowds, and in some ways I still do.

Because I found myself feeling afraid of what people would think of me, I often decided to take the risk out of a situation by just going off to read somewhere instead. This had a profound effect on me. It meant that I read widely, and soon found myself running out of books to read at my age level. At seven, I was reading books meant for eleven- or twelve-year-olds. While this really helped me with my English classes and creative writing, it didn't help at all in my quest to fit in. I gave up that goal pretty quickly.

I decided that if people wouldn't come to me, then I would get by without them. I had my books, and I could always relate to the characters in them. One of my favourite series of novels was *Tim and the Hidden People* by Sheila McCullagh. I had a lot of sympathy with the main character. Like Tim, I also had my own little world.

In my early years at primary school, I often ran round the playground pretending I was driving a bus. Although my father was a bus driver for some of my childhood, I'm not sure that I was deliberately trying to emulate him. Instead, I was enjoying playing in an alternative world, interacting with imaginary people who were getting on and off my bus—people who saw me as "normal."

"A single to Staple Hill," my imaginary passenger would say. I would hand him his change, issue his ticket, and wait for another passenger.

"Return to Temple Meads, please."

"I'm sorry," I'd reply. "You're on the wrong bus—you'll need the 51 bus on the other side of the road."

"Oh, okay." And the passenger would get off the bus.

To everyone else on the playground, I looked anything but normal. Here I was, this skinny runt, running round with an imaginary steering wheel—and being a bus, it was a *huge* steering wheel. I'd use my hands as the doors, too, and pretend to operate opening and shutting them. I would also make the noises the bus made.

It might seem obvious why I was bullied. At the time, though, this was how I dealt with being alone. To my mind, I was interacting with people; they just weren't real. Of course, this did little to help me interact with the people who *were* real. People getting onto my "bus" weren't going to argue with me, nor were they going to thump me, kick me, or call me names, which is what I ended up dealing with.

To make a bad situation worse, I wasn't helped by my tendency to be combative when challenged. Sometimes I acted like the whole world was against me, and that's how it felt at times. When the other children shouted and screamed at me, I resisted for quite some time, but in the end I gave in and had a go back at them. The children who were goading me were having great fun at my expense, knowing that if they kept going long enough, I would react.

The teachers constantly told me to ignore the bullying, telling me it would "go away." I refused to believe them but carried on trying not to react—and failed. Eventually I learned that shouting the odds back didn't actually help matters at all.

But even then I didn't know how to apply the teachers' advice in the right way.

When faced with children who were physically bullying me, I didn't know how to respond. Following the teachers' advice, I allowed the bullies to do what they wanted without taking any action to stop them. I tried to "ignore" the boys while I was being physically beaten, sometimes eight of them at a time in a lane on my way home. I was so outnumbered in such situations that it didn't matter whether I followed the teachers' advice or not.

Often the main troublemakers were waiting for me in certain parts of the playground, or in the alleyways after school had finished. I constantly tried to change the route I took going home from school, because Dorian, the main bully, would lie in wait for me. As he lived right by the school, he was virtually impossible to avoid. Sometimes I walked a mile out of the way in order to dodge the bullies, but this wasn't always possible. In these situations, I learned to just take the physical abuse.

I received emphatic and open threats that if I told anybody about what was going on the beatings would just get worse. So I tried to keep it to myself, but eventually I ran out of ways to explain away the bruises to my parents. Mum has always been a gentle soul, and she wanted to have a word with the school about it. My father had a different take on things: when we had disagreements, he sometimes told me it was "no wonder you get bullied." He apologised afterwards for saying it, but even though he didn't mean it, I took his words to heart. I could be argumentative at times, and especially with my father.

Mum did go and speak to the school about it. But as the bullies warned, it only made the situation worse. In the end, I just told myself I'd have to live with it.

At first this seemed the same as ignoring it. Other children had the outlet of their friends to moan to about people they didn't like, or who didn't like them. I didn't have that outlet, and could only take it in on myself. I didn't understand why the children were being nasty to me, and I didn't like things I couldn't understand. It left me feeling alone and powerless, and was the start of my bottling up my emotions.

How supportive the school was on the bullying issue depended on whom Mum spoke to. I always got on really well with the head teacher, Mr. Luton, but his deputy, Mrs. Seaby, was a different animal altogether. For some reason, she was always hypercritical of any work I did, and upon reflection, it didn't help that I was too defensive when she criticised my work.

One of the ways I attempted to avoid the bullying was to get myself a position as one of the helpers for the dinner (lunch) ladies. A group of four of us, including Alex, helped clear up after dinner. It helped keep me away from the playground, which was the last place I wanted to be.

There were other benefits to being a helper. We didn't get paid, but it was seen as a privilege and usually meant we had the best pick of the food. One dish more than any other was popular with every child at the school: chocolate shortbread with chocolate coating and chocolate custard. It tended to be so crispy that you almost needed a hammer and chisel to break it apart. As a result, we called it "chocolate concrete." That doesn't make it sound at all appealing, but it was the best thing ever served.

It was so popular that even children who normally brought in packed lunches would have school dinners on that day. By helping the dinner ladies, we were guaranteed a slice, and often were allowed to join the head of the queue. At Christmas we were all given a box of chocolates. So all in all, it was a great position to have.

That is, until the day one of the other boys started messing about. One of them wrote *prunes* in big letters on the dry wipe board. A few minutes later, Mrs. Seaby left her classroom and saw the writing. Immediately, she called us over and was quick to pick me out.

"What on earth do you think you are playing at, Potts?" she asked.

It was like the incident with Mrs. Hunt all over again.

"It wasn't me, miss," I said. "I didn't write anything."

"Of course it was you," she snapped. "I can recognize your scruffy handwriting a mile off."

This time, the boy who had done the writing owned up. Mrs. Seaby, though, was having none of it.

"It's no use trying to save your friend," she continued. "It's Potts's scruffy writing, and it's Potts who will pay." She turned to me. "You clearly can't be trusted to be a helper. You leave me no choice but to remove you from your position."

I was bitterly disappointed. Not just because of the injustice, but because the playground was the last place I wanted to be. When I wasn't avoiding the main troublemakers, I sat by myself on the steps watching all the other children having fun playing football and running round in groups. The playground showed me just how alone I was.

The playground bullies were given further ammunition by the prominence in the media of the Cambodian dictator Pol Pot. *Blue Peter*, a long-running children's TV series that aired twice a week on the BBC, was famous for its annual collection of silver foil and milk bottle tops to raise money for poorer parts of the world. They would recycle the metal in the tops and the money raised from this went to charity. This one year, it was for the people and children of Cambodia. Pictures were shown of the incidents there, and while young viewers were spared the gory details, we were left in no doubt that awful things were happening, and that we were to send in our foil and bottle tops as soon as possible.

The similarity of my name and that of Pol Pot was not lost on the bullies at Chester Park. Many found it hilarious that my parents "could have named" me that. I didn't want to just back down, so I tried to be the clever one by arguing with them and asking exactly how my parents were supposed to know in advance about something happening eight years after I was born. This just made them laugh more, and I was targeted with increasing frequency. I was reminded every day that "my" deeds meant that millions of people had to send their milk bottle tops off.

I wanted the other children to like me, but it felt like such an impossible task. I thought about taking things into my own hands. At Chester Park, in the junior section, there was a steep set of steps that led to the children's toilets. I would stand at the top of the steps and will myself to throw myself down. I could never bring myself to do it.

Having failed to throw myself down the steps, I came up with another idea. At the other side of the playground were temporary buildings called annexes. The section of the playground by the annexes had a five-metre metal bar going across from close to the annexes, about five inches off the ground. I decided to run round the section and tried to make myself trip over it hard enough to injure myself.

I knew what I was trying to do. I wasn't trying to kill myself, because that wouldn't achieve anything. I wanted to injure myself enough to get people to feel sorry for me. Enough to find myself in hospital for at least a few days. Now, I was bright enough to know this wouldn't be enough to make people like me, but I just wanted the other children to feel something other than hatred for me, even if it was temporary. Anything was better than being the most hated child at school.

Despite the best efforts of the bullies, there were other elements of early school life that I did enjoy. In the final year of primary school, my favourite teacher—the head teacher, Mr. Luton— organized a trip to Dieppe in northern France.

This was the first time I had ever been away from home without my parents. It also meant that I was the first child in my family to go abroad. Dad was in the Territorial Army for our early years, so he was sometimes away in Germany around the town of Hildesheim, close to Hanover. But apart from that and a trip my mum had made to Switzerland when she was at school, I was the only one to go abroad.

The trip took place in the autumn. We took a long ride in a coach to Newhaven in Sussex for our ferry crossing to Dieppe. In those days, you could travel within Europe without an individual passport, and we all travelled on a group one. The purpose of the trip was largely historical. We explored the area, learning about the ill-fated assault on the Dieppe cliffs during the Second World War. It was a pretty little city, flat and easy to walk round. The beaches were flat and the weather was sunny, if a little breezy and cold.

The trip was an adventure for me, and one that I felt privileged to be on. I remember falling asleep on the coach, curled up in my individual seat until we arrived back in the late evening. The whole excursion was a thoroughly enjoyable one—and was where my love of history was born.

I was also reasonably successful at sport in primary school. The one benefit of being bullied was that I got used to being able to run away, something I was generally very good at. I also had a competitive streak: just as I hated being wrong, I also hated being last. I got so competitive in the school sports day that I was disqualified from the egg and spoon race—that I had won—because I was deemed to have been *holding* the egg in the spoon rather than balancing it. I did okay in the sack race, finishing third. At least I wasn't disqualified! I did fall a few times, as jumping inside a sack as quickly as you can is much harder than it looks.

Of course, the happiest memories of school life were the holidays—those long summer weeks with nothing to do. My childhood was an era when package holidays abroad were starting to become commonplace for many families. Classmates would return after the long summer holiday to tell us about their escapades. I listened with envy about the sunny climes, the beaches, and the exotic food. My family didn't have the money for holidays abroad, and I was often teased about this at school.

The teasing, though, was misplaced, as I enjoyed our family holidays in the UK. Sometimes we'd go to Wales, staying at caravan parks in Prestatyn in North Wales and Newquay in West Wales. More often than not, however, we'd go to Portsmouth and Southsea. We never really knew why we liked the area so much; we just did. We always said it never rained when we went on holiday, and we usually came back with suntans. We associated it with happy experiences and sunny weather.

One year, Mum was working at a factory that made fireproof uniforms for firemen; she wasn't able to join us because she couldn't get time off. We got a letter explaining that someone we liked was going to meet us by our normal swimming spot. We had no idea who it was going to be. It was Mum. She had decided to surprise us by turning up unannounced on her day off. She could only stay for the day, and had to return on the train before joining us for the second week. This made that week very special.

Over the years, Portsmouth became like our second home. We spent a total of fourteen summers there. We usually stayed in a static caravan (mobile home) at the Eastern Road caravan park on the very edge of Portsea Island. It was fairly large and right by the sea. There were shower blocks and toilets for use by those who were camping. It was a four-mile walk to the Southsea seashore from the caravan park. We walked into Southsea and went to a regular area just west of South Parade Pier, between the pier and Southsea Castle.

Our trips to Portsmouth were by train on a bank holiday. We got the first service out from Bristol in the morning, which was around five o'clock. We took the very first bus to Old Market and then walked the half-mile down to Temple Meads station. It was still dark, and as Courage Breweries were still brewing in Bristol at the time, our nostrils were assaulted by the aroma of the hops being cooked along the River Avon. That bittersweet smell is something I still associate with my childhood.

It didn't bother us too much, though, as it was part of the passage to Portsmouth. We got there early enough to have break-fast in our favorite café by the station, and then walk down to the seafront. The walk to the beach was like walking through any suburb of any city, but to us it led to our wonderland. On the way home, we took the last train back from Portsmouth Harbour station, often called the "milk train," from the days when the last train of the day towed a few tankers of milk. Other parts of the country had the "strawberry train" with a similar setup. Even now, when I go somewhere for leisure, I try to get the first transport up and the last one returning, to make the most of the journey.

Southsea has a pebble beach, so swimming can be uncom-fortable when the tide is in, although when the tide is out you can walk into the sea and have sand between your toes. Pebble beaches do have one compensation, though: you don't have that awkward job of trying to get your shoes back on without getting them wet while trying to ensure you don't get a load of sand in them, either. On the other hand, when you get out of the sea onto a pebble beach, your skin is softened and those pebbles hurt!

We would spend the whole day at the same spot, having brought a packed lunch with us. It would usually be sandwiches filled with cheese or ham. Because it was a pebble beach, we couldn't play beach sports. We would swim for hours in the sea and then sunbathe for a few more hours. After a few hours' swimming, we had not only the smell of the saltwater but the salt itself once we had dried in the warm sunshine. This was all before people became concerned about skin cancer and being in the sun during the middle of the day. I had a tendency to burn with my first contact with the sun each year, but then I became a golden brown, something Mum was jealous about. That still holds true today, but obviously I do use sun cream now! People we knew didn't believe we had gone only ninety miles away from home, rather than Spain, because of our tans.

Towards the end of the day, we would pack up our things and walk down to Clarence Pier, which had the main funfair. We usually just wandered round and thought about which rides we would like to go on, not being able to afford any. We'd watch others having a good time and maybe have a cone of chips (french fries).

At times, there would be arguments amongst all four of us that would lead to threats of going home. Tony and Jane would often stick together; not surprising, their being twins. John and I would sometimes come to blows. Jane, however, always knew how to scheme and was too clever for us at these times: she would strike first, hitting when one of us was out of sight, and then stand where we could all be seen.

"Don't hit your sister!" bellowed Dad.

"But she hit me first!" answered whoever had hit her back. (We had full equality; if she hit any of us, then we would hit back, though never as hard as she had hit us.)

"I don't care, you don't hit girls!"

I'm not sure who said it, but out of the blue came the words, "But Dad, she's not a girl, she's my sister."

It took us a while to learn the lesson. I think Jane caught every single one of us out at least once. Jane and I still laugh about this now.

John's birthday always fell during the holidays, so we had a treat on that night by visiting the fair and having a go on the rides. The one we feared the most was the White Mouse: it was the most scary roller-coaster ride in the fair, and you got a good view of the sea on your way round. It was strange how John often suffered from travel sickness in the car, but he had no issues at all with the roller coaster. The fair was noisy but exciting, and we were surrounded by the smells of chips and vinegar. As it was John's birthday, we all got treated with a fish and chip supper, and then got on the bus back to the Eastern Road campsite.

Occasionally, we used the car and drove further up the coast to Hayling Island, Worthing, and Brighton. We liked Hayling Island the most, as it had a sandy beach, so we could use our buckets and spades. Even the pebble beaches kept us occupied, though, as I learned to skim stones there. It was something I always found relaxing. The secret to a six- or sevenfold skim lies in the choice of stone. Not too big, not too small, with a reasonable density so it won't be thrown off course by a wave. Then it's all about the speed of your throw and the angle at which the stone hits the water.

One of the highlights of Portsmouth in August was the Navy Days at the historic dockyard. They started out many years ago as a recruitment exercise for the Royal Navy—the modern equivalent of press-ganging! We always timed our holiday to coincide with the Navy Days weekend, because for a single entry price you could wander round most of the dockyard and go on board the ships. One of the major attractions was the aircraft carriers, and there were always long queues to see them. The only year when there weren't real Navy Days was 1982, because this was the year of the Falklands War between the UK and Argentina over the sovereignty of the Falkland Islands. It was very poignant to see the badly damaged HMS *Glamorgan* in dry dock after it had been hit by an Exocet missile, where several crew members were killed and injured. There were regular parades by the sailors, and the day ended with the rousing sounds of the Royal Marines Band playing the "Last Post."

Those days of wandering round the dockyards stirred us, though, and John and I vowed that we would join the navy when we were old enough. When we got home, we joined TS *Adventure*, one of the Sea Cadet Corps in Bristol. I planned to be an artificer, or engineer; an aim doomed by my lack of ability in physics and mathematics, which were prerequisites for the job. John, though, was more successful and a number of years later he joined the navy as a cook. He ended up serving for around twenty years, seeing much of the world and also serving in dangerous times such as Operation Desert Storm.

The Portsmouth holiday in 1982 doesn't just stick in my mind because of the Falklands War. I was eleven, leaving Chester Park for the big bad world of secondary education. Primary school had left me feeling confused. I hadn't known how to interact with the other children when I started, and upon leaving I felt like I knew even less about it.

The thought of going to secondary school scared me witless. I didn't see these new experiences as an opportunity but as a threat. Those six weeks of summer holiday in 1982 passed all too quickly, as I worried about being thrown into a new world I didn't know how to deal with. The one thing that had helped me cope with my problems in primary school had been my love of music and singing. In secondary school, I was going to need that solace more than ever.

CHAPTER THREE

Singing

I WILL ALWAYS remember the first time I experienced music properly. I was five years old, and was attending a service at our local church: All Saints, Fishponds on the northeastern side of Bristol. I was part of the congregation, standing up to sing a hymn, when I was suddenly taken by the sound of everyone singing together. It was such a beautiful, sweet sound that it took me out of myself. I was completely caught up in the moment. I'd heard music before, of course, but this was the first time I "got" it and realised just how special it was.

I soon discovered that not only was music something magical, but also that I was naturally good at it. I had an innate ability to remember tunes in my head, something that is often described as learning music by ear. I could hear a tune in church and sing it back with little effort, and also play it on the piano. Right from the start, I realised music was going to be an important part of my life.

When children at church reached the age of seven, they were

expected to start Sunday school. I had been singing in the church choir for a year by this point, and I wanted to continue singing rather than go to Sunday school. I couldn't do both, as they were scheduled at the same time. It took a little negotiation from my parents for me to be excused, but I got my wish. I was joined as a chorister by my brother John. Tony joined a different choir at St John's Church by our school. Jane wasn't interested in being in the choir, as she liked Sunday school. We were paid a small amount of money for weddings and normal services. It wasn't much, but it did give us something to save up and spend at the fair on holiday.

I wasn't sure why music made me feel good; I just knew it did. Seeing that the vicar did lots of singing during the service, for a while I wanted to be one. It wasn't because I had a calling; I thought it meant I would get to sing!

Even at an early stage, I gained a reputation for singing loudly. I sang tunefully, but always at full volume. This wasn't from being disobedient or wanting to show off, but simply because I enjoyed it. I was so loud that if I was in the congregation at a different church, I'd often turn heads as people could hear me from the very front of even a pretty large building.

One Sunday at home, I decided to experiment with some matches and paper. I think it was more about curiosity than anything else. I set the paper alight in a drawer in the bedroom I shared with my two brothers, and the smell and smoke made its way downstairs. Predictably I was caught and told by Dad to pray to God for forgiveness at church that evening. I was offered a choice of punishments: either I could miss a whole week's activities, namely Boys' Brigade, Cub Scouts, and choir practice; or miss the Cub Scouts camping trip to Exmoor a few months later. I really wanted to go camping, so I chose the week of missed activity instead.

That evening at evensong, I dutifully prayed for forgiveness as told to by Dad. To his surprise, I came home full of joy.

"Well," I said to my parents, "God forgave me!"

Dad looked startled. "What makes you say that?" he asked.

"We got a pay rise this evening!"

One thing I wanted from an early age was the opportunity to sing solo. I remember watching the BBC show *Jim'll Fix It* as an eight-year-old, and seeing a boy treble who had written to ask to sing in St. Paul's Cathedral. I was green with envy. I wanted to sing solo, and I dreamed of doing so in a huge church like St. Paul's. I didn't enjoy watching someone else doing it when it could—and should—have been me.

I eventually got my chance in a much smaller venue. A small choir made up of pupils was formed at my primary school, the majority of whom were girls. The choir only really performed publicly once a year at the school's carol service at St. John's Church, which was next to the school. In December 1978, I was asked to sing the first verse of "Once in Royal David's City" without accompaniment. This both excited and filled me with fear. It was a huge moment for me, and I still remember my legs feeling like jelly as I was singing, nerves being something that would always be with me.

Nineteen eighty was a key year in my vocal development. We had noticed in the local newspaper, the *Bristol Evening Post*, that one of the central Bristol churches—the great Georgian church, Christ Church with St. Ewen—was auditioning for boy choristers. It seemed too good an opportunity to miss, and I decided to audition.

The audition itself was a quiet affair in front of the organist and choirmaster, Brian Bussell and his deputy, David Moon. Mr. Bussell was a man with a jolly disposition and a fairly even temperament. But standing in the church in front of the panel, initially he looked domineering. Middle aged and almost bald, he was friendly, but you knew he was in charge.

My audition was successful, and I was selected to join the choir and be paid £200 a year plus bus fare expenses. I was thrilled. Christ Church wasn't large, but it had a long choral tradition supported by a benefactor who had left a large amount of money in her will, which paid for the choristers' annual fees.

At my first service in the choir, the whole of my family was present, including John, Jane, and Tony. John was heard singing by one of the church wardens and was subsequently invited to join. I was a little put out that I'd had to audition, but I was happy to be there, especially as I started getting solos.

New boys were always taken to All Saints Church in the parish for a fairly mild initiation. The church was said to be haunted by a monk who died defending the building's treasures at the time of Henry VIII's dissolution of the monasteries in Britain. We all had to stand up against a door while a few boys stood round the corner making shrieking noises, pretending to be the ghost.

My older brother and I had good fun in the choir and made friends. One particular Thursday there was a storm under way.

Having arrived early, John was running round with a few of the others, and he turned and said, "If I have ever told a lie, may God strike me down!" At that moment there was a huge flash of lightning and a rumble of thunder immediately after. He was petrified, but I laughed my head off.

As choristers we were well treated by the church. In addition to the income that covered our expenses and also helped pay for singing lessons, we had regular trips. We also had an annual meal out just before Christmas. This was a rare event indeed for me. We usually went to the Berni Inn on Broad Street, which was a huge treat. We were allowed anything we wanted on the menu, and as it was a steakhouse and not something our family could ordinarily afford, I was nervous about ordering anything expensive. Seeing my discomfort, Mr. Bussell told me to go for it. I ended up having (as did every other choir boy) a three-course meal of breaded mushrooms, rump steak, and ice cream for afters. We were given liqueur coffees at the end (minus the liqueur, of course), and felt thoroughly spoilt.

Christmas was one of my favourite times of the year at Christ Church. The smallness of the church meant the smell of incense filled it quickly. Carols by candlelight meant that the soft light shimmered from our white surplices and made our blue cassocks contrast with the stark whiteness of the walls.

I enjoyed singing the descants and being allowed to sing high and loud without getting into trouble for it. My favourite descant of them all was the one for "Hark, the Herald Angels Sing" because it was fairly long and pretty high.

The most special service of all was midnight mass on Christmas Eve. It wasn't just because this service was held so late at night and in the centre of Bristol, very close to the main clubbing area. (This resulted in plenty of drunks walking in; most of them harmless, happy drunks who overenthusiastically joined in the carols.) There was always a special atmosphere in the church on Christmas Eve. The smell of incense was particularly pungent, but it was balanced with the smell and light of the candles and the soft tones of the priest singing the responses. It was the only time of the year when the priest encouraged everyone to shake hands and wish each other "Happy Christmas." In this service, we would have *all* the best carols with *all* the best descants.

My other favourite time of year was around Easter. Passiontide, the approach to Good Friday and Easter, was always very poignant. On Maundy Thursday, the day before Good Friday, the candles were extinguished and the altar stripped. It made things very eerie and made me feel quite alone. In contrast, Good Friday was a busy singing day at the church, so it was always one of my favourites.

On alternate years, we would perform John Stainer's *Crucifixion* and Theodore Dubois's *Seven Last Words of Christ.* Each had its own attraction. Stainer's work was fairly typical Victorian English music, with rousing choruses and a few good solos for the adults (alas, nothing for the boy trebles), whereas Dubois's work, which I preferred, was more emotional.

I enjoyed my time at Christ Church. I more or less got on with the other boys in the choir, which felt like a dream come true. This helped reassure me that my voice was my friend. It was only when I was singing that I felt I had no enemies, so I embraced it. The only problem was that I'd get so caught up in the music that I forgot about the rest of the choir. It didn't matter how many there were, be it the twenty-five others at Christ Church (including adult singers) or a massed choir at Bristol's Colston Hall. I could always be heard.

This would often get me into trouble with our choirmaster, Mr. Bussell. Sometimes I would come into the church for evensong and find myself summoned to Mr. Bussell in the organ loft. I'd have to spend the whole of evensong sitting in a chair by the huge historic organ. While it was fascinating to watch Mr. Bussell playing Widor's Toccata at the end of the service, I much preferred singing back on the ground level. I was told to listen to the choir without me to hear how united it was. I would try to contain myself, but would find myself back up in the organ loft every six weeks or so, being given exactly the same lesson.

Mr. Bussell was a jovial man with a good heart, though he wasn't afraid of showing his displeasure. You could sometimes tell his mood by what he played as the recessional voluntary as we returned to the choir vestry. If it was Widor's Toccata (one of my favourites), then it usually meant he was in a good mood. If it was J. S. Bach's Toccata (which always sounded like something from a horror movie), then we knew we were in line for a telling-off.

Mr. Bussell very rarely raised his voice, but you always knew when he was unhappy. When he got really cross, he'd use a tactic that was effective to the nth degree: he would threaten us with the prospect of introducing girls into the choir. We were bright enough to know what this would mean. There was only space for fifteen or sixteen boys at most in the front pew of the choir stalls. Having girls in the choir meant redundancy for some of us, so it was a very effective threat indeed.

Singing

Despite spending a considerable amount of time banished to the organ loft, I got on well with Mr. Bussell. He was usually funny and pleasant, and towards the end of my time with the choir, he told me that I was one of the best choristers he had ever had the pleasure of working with. For me this was very high praise indeed, and made me feel very happy.

The money I earned from being in the choir paid for me to have singing and piano lessons. My teacher Miss Wilcox taught in her home in the Soundwell area of Kingswood, an affluent area on the edge of Bristol. I had to get a bus to and from lessons twice a week. She had many talented pupils, some of whom I remained friends with years later. Miss Wilcox was advanced in years and had a reputation for having a bad temper. She was so scary that she filled even her pupils' parents with fear. She was in her eighties and spoke with very authoritarian tones. She didn't suffer fools gladly, and though largely immobile in her seat, could certainly move her arms very well.

One Monday evening, for example, I had left late after my singing lesson and there was a risk of missing the bus. Fortunately, that was running late, too, and I ran to the bus stop just in time to catch it. I was getting on the bus when I was grabbed by the father of one of the other pupils, Chris Gammon.

"Come on," said Mr. Gammon. "I've got to give you a lift home."

"Don't be silly," I replied. "The bus is here now, and you only live round the corner."

"Oi!" the bus driver shouted. "Are you getting on or not?"

"He's not," said Mr. Gammon, pulling me back onto the

BEGINNINGS

street. "Miss Wilcox," he explained, as the bus drove away, "told me I had to drive you home."

His face was as white as a sheet: he was petrified.

This wasn't a rare emotion in Miss Wilcox's presence; she was mistress of all she purveyed.

Miss Wilcox was a hard taskmaster. My singing was far better than my piano playing, and I was always a little lazy with my piano practising. It generally showed when Miss Wilcox asked me to play the pieces she had given me to practise. She would get more and more frustrated with me, and wasn't afraid of showing it. I tried to make excuses, saying that our piano at home was out of tune. Rather than just accepting that, Miss Wilcox sent her piano tuner to our house to test our piano.

Miss Wilcox had another tactic, too. She decided that corporal punishment would make me perform better. After several weeks of playing badly and not really making progress, she picked up a garden cane and started rapping my fingers with it whenever I made a mistake. The more mistakes I made, the harder she hit me. I can see now that having sent a piano tuner at her own expense to look at my piano meant she was very passionate about music and wanted to ensure that we played as well as we could. Unfortunately, her plan had the opposite effect: the caning on the fingers was too much for me and made me give up studying the piano. I didn't tell my parents about the caning. I just told them I didn't want to play any longer. I felt that if I told the truth, I would just get into trouble for not practising. I cut my losses, as I knew I would never be a great pianist.

I can say one thing: I am very happy that Miss Wilcox didn't use the same tactics to correct my mistakes in singing! I did practise more and made fewer errors, but my singing was always more natural, and at times completely effortless. If I hadn't been doing well, I know she would have told me. My younger brother, Tony, was put off from having lessons with her, as she constantly told him off for sounding like he was chewing gum while he was singing. Miss Wilcox certainly didn't hold back!

My first crush was on one of Miss Wilcox's pupils. Her name was Angela Huggins, and she was everything a pre-pubescent boy wanted in a girl: tall (which I most definitely wasn't), pretty with wavy curls of blonde hair, and she lived in a fairly well-to-do area. I tried to sing like her, which got her to giggle at me.

What was to end any hope of a relationship with Angela (apart from her being a few years older than me) was my pretending we had got engaged (at my tender age of ten, this would have been a little extreme). Alex, my friend at school, and I went off for the day without telling our parents where we were going.

Alex had told his mum we were going to meet up with Angela, when in fact we did nothing of the sort. We were away from home much longer than I had told my mum. Worried, Mum phoned Angela's mum to find out where we were, and our cover was blown. I was too embarrassed to even speak to Angela after that.

I made good progress with my singing and was selected to represent the class at local music competitions. I performed with some success at Staple Hill Eisteddfod, Longwell Green Festival, and Kingswood, as well as taking part once or twice at the Bristol Eisteddfod, which was seen as the pinnacle of local competition. These competitions were cold, calculated affairs, and I didn't always enjoy them. The audience was usually made up of your competitors and their families, and there was a panel of three people who would listen and tell you what they thought. It was sterile and difficult, not to mention nerve inducing.

Mum would always come with me to the competitions to give me her support, and often Jane and Tony would come, too. Tony also tried a few competitions but found nerves difficult to deal with. Dad was rarely available to watch me perform, although he would come when he could. He made a point of watching me at the prize-giving concerts that followed the competitions. He would make up for missing these competitions in years to come.

I struggled to get anywhere at the Bristol Eisteddfod, usually scoring enough to get honours, but the best I ever did was to finish third. I generally did better at Staple Hill, where I won a couple of medals. At one eisteddfod there, I caught the eye of the master of choristers for the Bristol Cathedral, who told my mum and me that he was very keen to have me in the choir.

To be a chorister at Bristol Cathedral you had to go to the cathedral school. In fact, I had taken the entrance examination for the chorister's scholarship the year before, but it required me to go into secondary school a year early. I did reasonably well in all subjects, particularly English (as reflected from my advanced reading comprehension), but was not quite good enough at mathematics, so I wasn't selected. I was offered the opportunity to progress if my parents paid my fees, but since we didn't have the money for this, it was not to be. The master of choristers expressed his disappointment that I would be unable to join. I was disappointed, too. Singing at your local cathedral was the pinnacle for any chorister.

As much as I enjoyed singing, I hated competing. The competitive element made me feel terrible. Usually, I was fine until it was my turn to be called forward. At these sorts of events, you didn't have a waiting room. Instead, you were just called from the audience, watching every other singer before and after your own performance.

Everyone else sounded pitch perfect to me. I only had to waver a little to end up finishing last, and I always saw this as inevitable. I generally did better in the duet classes of the competition, where I usually competed with a boy my age named Craig. Craig was from a fairly well-to-do background and spoke and sang proper English, whereas my accent was always far more Bristolian. He would usually come away with a brace of trophies and medals, whereas despite being told by others that I was a better singer, I would come away empty-handed except for my duet with him.

Nerves often got the better of me. This was less of an issue at Staple Hill, which took place in the Methodist church. The large Victorian-style building had good acoustics, and was always pretty full during competitions. It had two levels, stalls, and a balcony, so it was not unlike a small theatre. My problem was when I was performing at smaller venues with fewer people attending, like at Longwell Green. I regularly failed to get even a merit there. I'd become nervous, and as a result my mind would go blank: I would forget the words in the middle of a song, even though I knew it backwards.

It was as if I feared singing to empty seats, since you cannot get feedback if no one is there. Singing was something I knew I was pretty good at, and as other parts of my life were less than ideal, I looked for approval. When I couldn't feel that approval, it left me feeling exposed and vulnerable. Under that pressure, I collapsed and my performance suffered.

It was around this time that I embraced classical music in a big way. This was largely thanks to watching the Steven Spielberg film *ET*. There was something about the music in the movie, alongside the scenes featuring a boy who wasn't fully accepted by his peers, that struck a chord, if you'll excuse the pun. I loved the feeling of the music washing over me, and I managed to get hold of an LP vinyl record of the London Symphony Orchestra playing the highlights of the soundtracks from *Close Encounters of the Third Kind*, *Star Wars*, and *ET*, all written by John Williams.

Listening to the record filled me with joy—so much so that I wanted to participate in the music, not just listen to it. Making sure no one could see me, I grabbed one of my mum's knitting needles and imagined it was a conductor's baton. This made me feel powerful, and I wanted to feel the emotion from the music more and more.

For my twelfth birthday, Mum and Dad bought me an inexpensive personal stereo. I got hold of some cassette tapes, and while one or two of them were pop, most of them were classical. I would invariably listen to them at full volume and would often be asked on the bus, "Would you mind turning your violins down, please?" This would usually get a few giggles from those around me.

I particularly enjoyed listening to the most dramatic music from classical composers. My favourites were pieces like Tchaikovsky's *1812 Overture*, Vaughan William's *A London Sym-*

phony, and Dvorak's *Symphony for Cello*. Most of these were with the Berlin Philharmonic Orchestra with Hebert von Karajan conducting.

My favourite orchestral piece was (and still is) Tchaikovsky's *Symphony No. 6*, the *Pathétique*. Its sadness grabbed hold of my heart and wrenched it so hard it wouldn't let go. I still remember the first time I ever listened to it. I was walking down Fishponds Road close to home, feeling the first movement reach into my psyche and resound with all the sadness I felt in life. It seemed to end with just the woodwind repeating the leitmotif that had been started by the strings. It ended calmly and quietly. I felt myself sigh with satisfaction and then . . . *BOOOOM!!!!* The full orchestra came in fortissimo. It was like a gun had gone off and I felt myself jump into the air, only just managing to land on my feet. Worse still, I had an audience. I was by a bus stop, and a double-decker bus had stopped right by me. There were some very wide eyes and some titters of laughter at the sight of me leaping into the air.

But that is what music did for me. It involved me heart and soul, and I got lost in it.

One event that happened while I was a chorister at Christ Church would affect me for many years to come. It was late May 1985, and I had just left choir practise. It was a little later than usual, and I would have to hurry to get to Baldwin Street to catch the bus, or I would be stuck waiting for over an hour for the next one.

Outside, the sky was fairly dark, although there was still some light left. It was also drizzling and damp; visibility was not good at all. I checked my watch; I would have to be quick, especially as the bus often left a few minutes early. I crossed Broad Street and sprinted down High Street, knowing that I only had a few minutes to cover nearly half a mile, and with a major road to navigate. However, I wasn't to make it that far. One minute I was running hard, but not out of breath. The next minute I was lying on the road in agony.

On High Street was one of the few original medieval buildings left from the bombing of the area during the Second World War, a half-timbered house from the sixteenth century. Work had been undertaken on the building, and scaffolding took up the vast majority of the pavement. I thought nothing of this, and ran between two pillars. There was no lighting on the scaffolding at all. As a result, I had no chance of seeing that the last section protruded diagonally across my path. I struck my head and mouth on the scaffolding, bleeding quite badly from the forehead.

The deputy choirmaster, Mr. Moon, had just left the church, and having seen the accident, ran over to help. I did my best not to show it, but I was in agony. Mr. Moon put me in his car and drove me to Bristol Royal Infirmary. I can only imagine how much of a mess I made in his car. There were two distinct injuries: I had a four-inch cut on the left side of my forehead that required fifteen stitches and left me looking like Frankenstein's monster. But the worst injury long term was to my mouth. I had hit the scaffolding with such force that my two front teeth were pushed into my gums and behind my nose, between my soft palate and nasal cavity. The resulting blood and pain were horrendous. Mr. Moon called home and waited for my mum to get to the hospital.

The doctor was able to stitch me up, but there was nothing

he could do about my teeth, apart from referring me to Bristol Dental Hospital the following day. The dentist there told me there was little even they could do, as the teeth would most likely return to position by themselves, though he didn't know whether the teeth would actually survive.

Over the next few weeks, the teeth did settle back into their correct position as the dentist suggested they might. All was not well, however. I had the most agonizing pain I'd ever experienced in my life, and the painkillers didn't deal with that. The nerves in my middle teeth were badly damaged and my teeth were killing themselves off. One of them—the same one I had hit on the subway wall when cycling on Alex's sister's bike—needed a full crown.

The cost of the crown would have been too expensive, but fortunately I was under the care of the emergency team at the dental hospital. On top of which, I was being treated by some of the prettiest female dental students the University of Bristol had to offer, so the accident had its compensations! I learned how to sit quietly for hours in the dental chair without complaining. I had to, as I wound up spending three hours in the chair every week for six months. Not only that, but local anaesthetic didn't affect me, and I could usually feel everything they were doing. I was offered free orthodontic treatment to deal with the fact that my bottom teeth were jumbled up and untidy, but to my eventual detriment, I declined due to the amount of time I was already spending in the chair.

I ended up having a long career as a chorister, and Christ Church became a second home for me. When we moved to Stoke Gifford on the edge of Bristol as part of my dad's job, getting to church got more complicated. John became a bit of a bad influence, and we skived off a few choir practises. It wasn't until 1987 that motions started to be made for me to leave Christ Church choir. I was a pensioner in chorister terms, as most boy trebles have their voices go funny around fourteen or fifteen. Here I was, at seventeen, still singing boy treble.

Some of my supporters in the church had raised a concern that by continuing to sing treble, my adult voice might be affected. I was given £50 in book tokens and thanked for my seven-plus years of service. I didn't want to leave. While I understood they were trying to act in my best interests, I felt disappointed. I didn't yet know what my adult voice would be like and was worried that I was leaving the professional world of singing behind me, perhaps forever.

CHAPTER FOUR

Secondary School Life

"SO WHERE are you going to secondary school, then, Potts?"

It was towards the end of my final year at primary school, and the playground bullies were taking an unexpected interest in my continued education.

"Whitefield," I replied, naming one of the local Fishponds secondary schools.

"Well, what do you know?" The bully rubbed his hands with glee. "I'm going there, too. Guess I'll be able to help you settle in, introduce you to some of the other pupils," he continued with a cackle. "See you after the summer holidays, then."

I watched the bully and his friends wander off, chuckling to themselves at the thought that they'd be able to continue tormenting me. I had a little chuckle to myself, too, as I watched them go. What they didn't know was that I wasn't going to Whitefield at all. Instead, like my siblings, I had a place at St. Mary

Redcliffe and Temple School in central Bristol, and the opportunity of a fresh start.

St. Mary Redcliffe was a partially voluntary funded church school, thought of locally as almost being a public school (the American equivalent of British *public school* is private school). Its academic reputation was high, and places there were highly sought after. In order to attend, you and your parents had to be baptised and go to church regularly: a document attesting to your regular church attendance had to be signed by your parish vicar or priest. Fortunately, my father was churchwarden at All Saints, so this was easily achieved.

My older brother, John, was already in the third year at St. Mary Redcliffe School and was one of the most popular children there. He knew how to play the social game at school and keep the bossiest personalities of the playground happy. On one occasion, John found a dead fox on the streets of Fishponds while doing his newspaper round, and ran home to get a bread knife to cut its tail off. He had various offers for the severed tail and eventually sold it to the person who offered the lowest amount. This might sound stupid, but the lowest offer came from one of the main kids in the third year. From that point on, he was in with the uppermost gang at school.

John knew how to get along at school in a way I did not. I saw my problems as my own, and I felt that if I got John to interfere, it might just make things worse for him. I had come through seven years of not knowing how to navigate the social currents, with only one "friend" who couldn't be relied on, so my interpersonal skills were limited, to say the least. So although I had the opportunity for a fresh start at secondary school, I didn't know how to take it.

I was bullied sporadically in my first two years at Redcliffe. In all honesty, I have to accept some responsibility for the reaction of my peers. I tried to absorb the teasing and attacks, but this wasn't always the best thing to do. I just bottled everything up until the inevitable explosion came. This was something the children at primary school were familiar with. I was timid most of the time, but capable of being one of the strongest children physically, if I had a paddy (a fit of anger); this was how one or two children described my explosions of temper, leading to them call me "Paddy Potts."

My biggest problem was thinking that admitting I was in the wrong, or being seen as being in the wrong, was a direct attack on me. I argued with the children who were teasing me, often reacting first and asking questions later. My house teacher, Mr. Pullin, took me aside and suggested I deal with it in a different way. He told me to ignore the situation; that it would go away if I did.

Once again, this was the mantra from the teachers and my parents. I tried very hard to follow their suggestions but was not always successful. I'd take it for so long, and then blow my top. I can see now how this was entertaining for those round me, especially those who were pushing my buttons. But at the time it was very difficult for me to deal with. I wanted to be liked, but I realized at the very start of my time at Redcliffe that it was very unlikely to happen.

* * *

Physical education should have been one of the best classes for me. I was one of the fastest runners in school, so I was picked to represent the school at cross-country running, a skill I kept up into my twenties. I would later represent my city and county at cross-country events round the country.

Games afternoons took place on Brislington School's playing fields. We would make our way on the coach to Brislington, an area on the edge of Bristol, and get changed into our red-and-black rugby tops and striped socks. We would start with a cross-country run that was generally completely flat, and then have a twenty-minute rugby match. Rugby was the school's main sport for boys; hockey was the main sport for girls.

I enjoyed the running and was always one of the first five to finish, but I hated the rugby. All through school it was a license to a beating. Whenever the ball was thrown at me, I would catch it and suddenly have eighteen boys piling on me in what was meant to be a ruck (huddle) of players attempting to get hold of the ball; it was actually a circle with me in the middle being repeatedly punched in the stomach, the ball having long been dropped on the ground. This was a regular occurrence throughout the first few years at Redcliffe, and I dreaded the games. I always hoped the rugby pitches (fields) would be waterlogged, meaning we would do a longer cross-country run instead.

I also hated the communal parts of sport such as changing and showering, as this was when the bullying was worst. With no adult supervision, the gang mentality was at its strongest. I would try to wait until the other boys had showered before having mine, and this was sometimes possible because PE was a double period before our break. Yet I was often pushed headfirst into the shower, completely naked, and kicked as everyone had a good laugh at my expense.

This happened so often that I got used to it. Sometimes it was "just" name calling. But sometimes I got a kicking. Sometimes a tie-flicking, often towards the groin, which as you can imagine was very painful. The tie would be flicked so hard that there was an audible "crack" as the tie flicked back. The worst thing was that the changing rooms didn't have a corner for me to hide in. I was exposed in more ways than one.

It was at the end of one the afternoon games sessions that I made my first real friend at Redcliffe. As usual, I didn't want to shower with the rest of the boys, so I waited to be the last in. As a result, when I got to the car park the coaches had already left.

There was another boy who had also missed the coach back: Nicholas. He was about the same height as me, with short black hair. Neither of us had enough money for a bus ticket to the centre of Bristol, so we were left with the daunting prospect of a four-mile walk to Temple Meads, where our bus passes were valid.

The sports fields were close to Verrechia's ice cream factory, which had a shop window close to the road, and Nick kindly bought me an ice cream for the long walk ahead. We started chatting, and became friends. Nick and I ended up spending quite a bit of time together after school, as we were both on the same bus route. He had the latest video games and a bike. He always shared these generously, even though I was never very good at playing computer games. I did okay at *Spy Hunter*, which was basic compared to today's games, but it led the market at the time. I can still hear the sound of the cassette tape now.

BEGINNINGS

The disparity between our backgrounds was never an issue because Nick's mother made sure he was considerate. He wound up being my longest-term and most reliable friend at Redcliffe.

For the most part, however, I struggled to fit in, and my house teacher's report told of me being "quarrelsome." Everyone else seemed to have made friends so much more easily. I did try to get along better with the other pupils, but it was still difficult for me. Whenever there was a large group I retreated to safety, as I always felt that the crowd was against me. My reading was still very advanced, and I retreated into that frequently. This meant that my comprehension level was also very advanced, and I always got great remarks from Mr. Pullin for English, with many good ideas culled from my reading.

Redcliffe was divided into "houses." They weren't physical houses: each floor of the main building was devoted to one house. They were named after different people, each a benefactor associated with the school. At the time I attended the school, first-year pupils were separated into James House. At James House, schooling was still quite old-fashioned. Discipline was firm, and corporal punishment was very much alive and well. If you were particularly naughty, you would end up in front of Mr. Graham, the stern head of house. Use of corporal punishment took the form of a beating from what was known as the "percy." It was an old Dunlop plimsoll, or trainer shoe, and those who received the beating spoke about it with awe. The rest of us tried to make sure we avoided that particular punishment.

From the second year onwards, we spent our time at the main school building in Somerset Square. It was a 1970s building with plenty of glass and concrete. I quickly gained a reputation with the teachers as being someone who could do very well when I applied myself. I was particularly good at English and German, and was usually at the top end of the class. I struggled more at mathematics and had to really apply myself very strictly at the sciences to make good progress.

I was relieved about one thing, though: that I wouldn't have to do any more needlework after the first year. I wasn't very good at it, and although it taught me how to sew a button, I didn't see any use for it. Instead, we did something called home economics, which involved planning meals and cooking. I actually enjoyed this, and made several different dishes including meringue, bread-and-butter pudding, and cottage pie. My favourite, though, was preparing mackerel. One Tuesday morning, we came in to find a mackerel at each of our work stations. We had to slice them open, gut them, and clean them out before stuffing them and baking them. This I loved doing, and it taught me to cook, which is something I still love to do.

By my third year, I was promoted to the top stream, as I had managed to improve my term-time work. My main problem was that I was never very organized and always did everything last minute. Contrary to what my teachers thought, it wasn't because of laziness, but rather disorganization. Not only that, I knew I tended to get my best work done when I was forced to do it in one go. This was how I always managed to get high grades in examinations. As a result, I tended to treat term-time work like exams and do it as the deadline loomed.

I often did my work on the bus to and from school. The bus would pass over many potholes and bumps, making my pen jump up and down, and as a result my writing was often pretty illegible. Many teachers talked about my pen not being able to keep up with my brain. Throughout school, I continued to frustrate my teachers by doing little in the way of homework, yet breezing through the exams.

The bullying became worse in my third year. One particular PE day, someone in the changing room pushed me onto the wet shower floor. Then he put his foot on my naked back and shouted, "Paul Potts is dead!" Everyone cheered. It was so loud that it was heard by the teachers in the gym, who shouted for me to hurry up and get ready.

I wished I *were* dead. At least that would make the other students happy. I would stand in the playground watching everyone else getting on with their lives and with those round them, and ask myself, Why me? What did I ever say or do to the others that made them hate me? During another PE lesson, while I was taking another beating, I asked them this very question.

"Why do you hate me so much? What is it I've done to you?"

They laughed even harder.

"We hate you because you're Paul Potts and you're alive!"

Things didn't get better when I tried to be helpful by returning a textbook that my older brother, John, hadn't returned. It was a physics textbook my class was using, and I thought I was doing a good turn. The physics teacher, Mr. Samphire, had other ideas and accused me of having stolen the book the previous week. I explained the situation, but unfortunately Mr. Samphire did not believe me and repeated the accusation in front of the whole class.

Because I continued to assert that I hadn't stolen it, I was told to stand outside the class for the remainder of the lesson.

It was a games afternoon, and I was one of the last to approach the buses to take us to Brislington. What greeted me was horrific. There were two fifty-five-seat buses full of other boys. Every boy on each coach stood up and shouted, "Thief! Thief! Thief!" pointing their fingers at me. I got on my bus and received the same treatment. What made matters worse was that Mr. Samphire was on my bus. While fifty boys were shouting at me, both he and the teacher next to him just chatted away as though nothing was happening. All I could do was sit and listen to the shouts, waiting for the boys to get bored with it. It took some time and left me feeling very low, especially as the teachers on both coaches did nothing to stop it.

It wasn't just verbal abuse that I had to take on an almost daily basis. The threat of violence always loomed over me every day of the week—before, during, and after school. Like at Chester Park, I tried to find different routes home, but this was difficult as quite a few of the bullies travelled on the same bus route as me.

I tried hanging around after the last class, but often a large group would wait for me to leave. The only exception was on Friday afternoons, as that was when the second school choir practise of the week was held, and it was over an hour long.

On a day that was designated as a wet day, we were allowed to stay in our house tutor rooms, which enabled me to avoid the bullying. Otherwise I was an easy target. Quite often some of the girls in my year would stand up for me, telling the boys to leave me alone. However, the boys dealt with this by saying, "Oh, you fancy him then, do you?" They'd turn on the girls and make fun of them, as if finding me attractive was a capital offence.

Many lunchtimes were punctuated by "mild" bullying—being thumped, kicked, and ridiculed—but often the bullying was very serious indeed. On one occasion, one of the unpleasant girls picked up a brick and threw it at my head, and I was only just able to dodge it. The boys found this hilarious, and gave the brick back to her so she could throw it again. She duly obliged, although with less accuracy this time, and I was able to escape by running away.

There were times when the attacks were truly malicious. On one occasion, one of the stronger boys grabbed me from behind, put me in a double armlock, and tried to push me through the science classroom windows. I managed to pull away, but not without gashing the back of my head on the corner of the open window. The four-inch cut required hospital treatment and several stitches.

Of course, I wasn't stupid enough to tell the teachers or my parents what actually happened. I had been warned of the consequences that would befall me if I did. I told the teachers I had been walking by the open window without looking and caught my head. All the time, the bully stood behind me acting like a concerned bystander. He was of course making sure I didn't tell the truth.

Some lunchtimes, I would find refuge in the music room. Wednesdays were an escape because that was the first school choir rehearsal of the week, but otherwise the music rooms were out of bounds. Rehearsals were also held after school on Fridays. I did manage to get a tacit agreement that I could be there from the head of the music department, Mr. Weaver, and from some of the girls who were choir monitors, and who became good friends of mine. This meant I could avoid the playground more often.

That aside, I never felt that the support from the teaching staff at Redcliffe was sufficient. Towards the end of my school career, the lack of support was more obvious. Once while I was being kicked in the back and my possessions thrown around, the teacher simply told me to take better care of my books, without a word to the boys who were throwing them.

This time, I did try to speak to the head of sixth form about the treatment I was getting. As usual, I was told to ignore it and not to react. In the end, speaking to the teachers about it led to a note on my locker saying that fifty students would wait for me at the end of the day, and I'd be in a coffin after they finished what they planned. I avoided school for two weeks. I didn't speak to my parents about the bullying or how it made me feel. This made me feel all the more alone, but I believed telling them meant I was admitting I was worthless. By not talking to anybody about it, neither my parents nor any other member of my family, I could pretend it wasn't happening.

Sitting back and taking the physical and mental bullying was to have a massive effect on me. I gave up on my personal appearance, which simply made the bullying worse. But I couldn't see any point whatsoever in caring about how I looked, because I knew it wouldn't make a difference in how I was treated. In fact, absorbing all the abuse made me feel like *I* didn't matter.

I wanted to end it all, but knew from primary school when I tried to fall down the stairs that I didn't have the nerve to go through with it. I was trapped in a world I didn't want to be part of—and there was worse to come.

On Tuesday and Friday evenings from the age of twelve, I went to Sea Cadets. This was like a junior version of the Royal Navy. My attendance resulted from our family's love of Portsmouth and our frequent trips to the Navy Days at Portsmouth Naval Base. John and Tony also attended, although Tony didn't appreciate Able Seaman Potts being in charge of his division.

We were based at Hotwells at TS *Adventure*, which was close to Cumberland Basin, the main entrance to Bristol Docks. It was what the navy calls a "stone frigate"; in other words, a building. It still had a mast, but this was for ceremonial purposes and parades.

Sea Cadets meant lots of "spit and polish," with John and me spending hours getting our hobnail boots reflecting like mirrors and our brass buckles shining like gold. Tuesday was cleaning day, and we would wear our No. 2 dress blue shirt and trousers. Friday was parade day, which meant wearing No. 1s: full sailor's rig jacket, bell-bottoms, lanyard, and collar, complete with white cap. Our outfits always drew a lot of attention when John and I got on the bus.

I had to work hard for my seamanship badge, as I wasn't that good at rope work. I found knots quite difficult, apart from the basic reef knot I had learned in cubs. But I persevered and eventually got my badge. This meant I was eligible to get my leading seaman's badge once I had passed the "at sea" course. The course involved a trip to Weymouth and a trip on an MFV, a merchant fishing vessel of Second World War vintage. The intention was to sail across the channel to Alderney and Jersey; we would all take turns to both steer the ship and look out for fishing buoys, which could get snagged in the ship's propellers.

When the time came for the trip, the seas were rough with force-seven gales. This meant that our journey to the Channel Islands would not happen. Our ship went up and down like a small bucket, which led to some cases of sea sickness. I wasn't bothered by the motion, being the only one of the Potts children who suffered no motion sickness. I found it quite amusing how the others were retching over the side.

I was fifteen at the time of the trip, and was going through the worst of the bullying at school. It was a five-day trip, and there were twelve boys on the course. Amongst the civilian helpers was a former Royal Navy captain from our unit, a man called Mr. Burton-Barri. I was one of the first to rise in the morning, and I always found Mr. Burton-Barri sitting in front of my bunk, watching me intently. He would say nothing except for a moody "morning." Mr. Burton-Barri was average height with greying hair and a similarly greying beard. He looked every bit the salty sea dog. Initially I thought nothing of his gazing, and assumed he was just waking himself up.

At the time, I had started smoking cigarettes sporadically, although I hadn't formed a habit. I didn't really inhale fully, and wasn't really sure why I had started other than the fact that John was smoking. On the trip, Mr. Burton-Barri started giving me a few cigarettes to smoke, which I saw as harmless, although I did notice that he only gave them to me. Over the next few days, he gave me so many cigarettes that it gave me a headache, and I stopped smoking as a result.

What I didn't notice, even though all the signals were there, was that I was being groomed. At the end of the week, Mr. Burton-Barri asked me if I would stay on for the day at the unit and help give the place a spring cleaning. For some reason, I didn't even react when Mr. Burton-Barri told me he had been warned about getting too involved with cadets. I should have walked away, but instead I was sucked into allowing him access to me that was both inappropriate and abusive.

It started with Mr. Burton-Barri sitting me on his knee in his office. I didn't know what was happening, or why it was happening. I just felt paralysed. Nobody saw, as it was only the two of us in the unit at the time. While he had me on his knee, he made a suggestive comment about having seen me get out of bed on the ship and thinking that I was excited around other boys. Then he kissed me on the lips. It didn't stop there. He found excuses to have me visit the uniform store, and there he kissed and touched me inappropriately. He touched my thighs and between my legs, grabbing my genitals but not getting the reaction he was looking for.

I never responded, physically or verbally. For me, *nothing* was happening. I didn't get "excited" and I didn't enjoy it. I tried to avoid getting myself into situations where we were alone, but he seemed not to be under any suspicion. I would be sent to the uniform store or to another part of the unit, and there he would touch me. I never objected and never stopped him; I just accepted it.

Why did I allow someone to touch me like this? I didn't want him to touch me at all. It made me feel guilty and dirty. I wanted to scream and shout, but no matter how hard I tried, no noise came out. I constantly beat myself up about it, asking myself how I could allow someone to do what he had done. But I did and said nothing, never telling him that his behaviour was inappropriate. I could have reported him, but I didn't. I didn't know whether I would be believed, and I thought that because I had never objected to him or told him to stop, it would be seen as my fault.

The touching and kissing went on sporadically for more than a year. I couldn't deal directly with what was happening. The way I dealt with it was to not show up to parades, and the longer time went on, the more I avoided going. Finally, it came to the attention of the commanding officer that I hadn't been for a few weeks. Here was my opportunity to come clean. I could tell him everything and explain why I hadn't been.

Did I do that? No. I made a lame excuse saying that we had moved to Filton as part of my father's work, and therefore it was difficult for us to get to the unit (he had become head caretaker at Filton High School at this time, and living on the premises was obligatory). Instead, I blamed myself for what I now understand was abuse. I felt that I had allowed him to do it. I was unclean. I was *nothing*. Therefore what happened didn't matter. Why? Because *I* didn't matter.

At the time all this was happening, the physical and mental abuse at school was at its worst. Being *told* I was worthless was one thing. Having over a hundred boys screaming obscenities at me, calling me names, and telling me I would be dead before the end of term was hard enough to take. Actions, though, speak louder than words. Wherever I went, people would touch me inappropriately, grab me or kick me between the legs, throw things at me, and throw *me* at things. I was something to ridicule, something to spit at. I wasn't a person at all.

I told no one about what was happening at Sea Cadets. There were many reasons for this. I didn't know whether anyone would actually believe me; it would have been my word against someone who had just been made an officer in a cadet force. There was also the fact that I had said and done nothing to oppose it. Most important, however, was the fact that the moment I told anyone, I was demonstrating not just to them but also to myself that I was nothing; even less than nothing.

Everything I was going through demonstrated that to me. All I could do was sit back and let it happen—I didn't have to enjoy it or take part in it. I did neither. From age fifteen to seventeen, what I wanted, what I didn't want, and what I felt seemed completely irrelevant. I was nothing more than a plaything for anyone who wanted to use me.

What happened to me at this time affected my future relationships. I always felt like a fraud when someone cared for me; it made me insecure and made me hold on too hard to those I cared about. I wanted to be loved. I wanted someone to care. But I felt that sooner or later, anyone who cared for me would find out that I was really nothing, and walk away.

Years later, when I met Julz for the first time, I crossed my fingers for luck and told her everything I'd gone through. I feared she would walk away. Instead, she held my hand and told me we would get through it together. I cannot express how lucky I am to have found her.

CHAPTER FIVE

Singing through the Pain

*T*HUD!

It had been a long morning at school when my concentration was interrupted by a loud thump to the right of me. Landing on the neighbouring desk was a board eraser, thrown with pinpoint accuracy. The eraser wasn't meant to hit my classmate Chris, but to bounce just in front of him, giving off a spectacular splash of chalk dust. I looked across at his blazer, which had gone from black to white, a telltale sign he hadn't been paying attention.

"Sorry, Chris, was I disturbing you?" said the teacher, Mr. Weaver, as he walked over to reclaim his eraser.

Mr. Weaver, or Phil as we were allowed to call him outside school, was my favourite teacher at Redcliffe. Not only was he a mean shot with a board rubber, he was also head of music.

"Sorry, sir," Chris said. "It won't happen again."

"Don't make me keep you behind. Not when there's choir practice later on." He looked at me with a friendly wink.

The school choir was the one steadfast thing amongst the chaos and heartache I went through. At times, it was the only thing that kept me going. Mr. Weaver worked us hard, and we had practice twice a week: Wednesday at lunchtime and Friday after school.

We had a varied repertoire and a packed diary of performances. Our main responsibility was to be the choir at the end and start of term services, house eucharists ("Eucharist" was the name for communion, which the school gave as a religious service at the start of every term), and special occasions like Ascension Day and the Colston Day service.

The latter was named after the Bristol benefactor Edward Colston, who cofounded the school in 1709. Colston Day was a celebration of the founding of Temple Colston School, which subsequently merged with the even older St. Mary Redcliffe School that went as far back as 1571. It was quite a privilege for us to be in the choir, because seats for the Colston service were allocated to three per tutor group across the school.

The Colston Day service had many advantages, and getting out of afternoon school and going home early was just one of them. There were two very traditional elements to the service. Each pupil was given a ten-pence piece and a Colston bun, which was a sticky bun with currants and sugar streusel pieces; the tradition went back to much earlier times when the gift was two shillings and a bun. The pastries were very popular, and there was an active trade amongst those who wanted an extra bun in exchange for the ten-pence piece.

The choir's busiest period was the approach to Christmas. We visited local elderly people's clubs and hospitals, singing carols and Christmas songs, and these events were always well received. I got to sing many more of the descants—higher melodies that acted as counterpoint to the main melody—that I had so loved performing at Christ Church. So much so that when I eventually started singing tenor in the choir towards the end of my school days, I carried on singing the descants, much to the consternation of the sopranos in front of me, who were used to taking that role themselves.

Singing liberated me. It didn't just make me feel happy; it made me feel complete. Whatever happened around me, at school or elsewhere, my singing made me feel like I made a difference. It seemed to make people smile. At special services and perform-ances, the whole of my family would come to watch. This helped me feel important at a time when I felt irrelevant.

In the run-up to Christmas, we also performed at Temple Meads, the entrance of the main railway station in Bristol. We raised money for local charities, amongst them St. Peter's Hospice and the homeless shelters. Here we received a more mixed response, ranging from generosity to rudeness: some commuters complained that we were "a bloody nuisance" standing in the way, and that they were going to miss their train.

The choir also performed at weddings and the occasional funeral. In my second year at Redcliffe, I was summoned to the headmaster's office. Thinking I was in trouble, I was worried as I was stood outside waiting for the light to turn green to enter. Instead, Mr. Eachus wanted to speak to me about an unusual proposition. He had been approached by an African group living in Bristol to find someone to sing at its prince's funeral. I was delighted and flattered that Mr. Eachus had thought of me. It was at a church in the Bedminster district of Bristol, and I was to sing the Samuel Sebastian Wesley anthem "Lead Me, Lord." It was a short service, and I got paid £20 for doing it. I put the money in with my savings from the paper round towards spending money for our next holiday.

As well as the Christmas bookings, one of the other main features of being in the choir was that we went on a number of special trips. Over my time at the school, I travelled with the choir all round mainland Britain.

In my first year we travelled by train to Winchester in Hampshire, where we were the guest choir at Winchester Cathedral. We left fairly early in the day and went straight to the cathedral for rehearsal. We were told that rehearsal would be finished by one in the afternoon, and that our parents should wait for us. It was here that I learned to take schedules with a pinch of salt. Musicians can be perfectionists, and Mr. Weaver kept us until nearly two o'clock. There was barely enough time for us to have lunch before we were due back to sing evening prayer, let alone have a wander round the city.

The medieval cathedral was a beautiful venue to sing in, and you could hear our voices reverberating round the church, which made me feel very proud. It was a grand building in keeping with Winchester's status as the capital of England in Saxon times. It had huge windows and a very long nave; in fact, we were informed by the verger that it was the largest nave in any cathedral in Europe. Yet I couldn't help feeling that we just didn't have enough time to see the sights and explore the city. After that, Mr. Weaver made a decision that we would no longer do a day trip for performances. In future, we would go away for a week to perform at cathedrals and local churches, as well as see quite a bit of the surrounding area. He felt that much of the day was wasted in travelling, and it would limit where we could perform if that had to be close by.

Our first tour took us to the pretty town of Skipton, in the scenic Yorkshire Dales, a four hours' drive north of Bristol. In order to go, I had to save up money from my paper round to pay for the trip, and Mum and Dad helped top it up. I was looking forward to the opportunity to sing in different venues and large cathedrals, and also to see the country.

Of course, on these tours there were no hotels. In fact, there weren't even beds! As well as a rucksack or suitcase, each choir member brought his own sleeping bag, and we slept on church floors. Many of the choir would also bring airbeds, and the sounds of snoring and the movement on rubber mattresses punctuated the night. My own sleeping bag went directly on the hard church floor.

We would travel together as a group on the train from Temple Meads, and Mr. Weaver had an ingenious way of keeping the cost of the trips down. He asked parents who had rail cards (cards that gave a 33 percent discount to adults, and up to four children free per adult) to give them to us, which greatly reduced our rail fare. We sat together and sang through our whole repertoire on the train, usually getting a lot of appreciation from the travelling public.

Most of our meals were eaten in the church we were staying in, but sometimes we would be given £1 for supper, and we'd take this to the local fish and chip shop get some chips, a drink, and perhaps a sausage. A pound went much further in 1984 than it does now! Everything we did, we did together; the washing up was done in turns by groups of students, and rotas were devised for sandwich-making duties. There were endless choices of sandwiches, from corned beef to tuna mayo, egg, or cheese.

There was a strong sense of community in the choir, which was a world apart from what I experienced outside it. In it, and especially on tour, I felt like I could *be* someone, rather than just some*thing* to ridicule. It was the perfect respite from the playground and all the horrors it held for me.

That first choir tour was an absolute revelation. I forged many friendships, several of which endure today. At one point, two friends, Ilena Bailey and Ruth Mould, sneaked into the boys' area in one of the halls to see two of the choirboys. In fact, Ruth is now married to the boy she sneaked in to see—one of my colleagues at Christ Church, Tim Day. Some of my longest-running friendships started on that tour.

It was a fun week, and we performed in Skipton Parish Church and also led evening prayer at beautiful York Minster. A few months after we had performed there, the south transept was struck by lightning and a huge fire destroyed the roof, including the many beautiful bosses, or wooden protrusions. We had been in that very transept waiting for our procession into the choir stalls only three months prior. Mr. Weaver took us on several day trips: one to Scarborough, and on another day, we also had a full day's walk in the wilds of the Yorkshire Dales. We also got a ride on the Settle and Carlisle steam train.

The following year, the choir tour took us to Margate, where I developed my first proper crush on a girl, Ilena Bailey, one of the girls who had snuck in to see the boys as I described earlier. Slim but not skinny, with long blonde hair, to me Ilena was the perfect girl. This made it all the more difficult for me to do anything about it. I was hopeless in situations like this, as I had no experience, and I always assumed that any girl I asked out would just say no. My shyness got in the way. Ilena made various comments that were very strong hints that I didn't act on. I fancied Ilena all the way through my time at Redcliffe, but never did anything about it. We were great friends throughout our school careers, however, so all was not lost.

The following year, the choir went to the beautiful Cornish resort of St. Ives, which has long been popular with artists, and for good reason. The scenery is stunning, and St. Ives has to be one of the best places in the world for a sunset. The tour was the first that my younger brother, Tony, participated in. On the first night, after a quick rehearsal, it was time to go to bed. The piano in the hall, which had seen better days and was horrendously out of tune, was on top of Tony's sleeping bag. Somehow it had been pushed there after our first rehearsal in the hall.

We tried to push it off, to no avail—or so we thought! Tony gave his sleeping bag a big haul and to his horror, the piano came away and went crashing to the floor with an almighty bang. Tony was shocked and upset, thinking he was going to get into trouble. But when Mr. Weaver walked in, he became red faced with laughter. As it turned out, the piano's fall did it a lot of good. It played much closer to being in tune, so perhaps Tony had done it a favour.

Our tour to North Wales was also a memorable one. We spent time in the town of Llandudno, again sleeping on the floor of the parish church. Supervision was fairly relaxed, and a huge group of us were walking along the Llandudno seafront singing at the top of our voices. It must have been strange to those in the hotels and guest houses to hear us singing *Godspell* as we strolled along. We had pooled our chip money, and one of the sixth formers went to get some beer. It wasn't exactly rock and roll; we didn't drink more than a can each, and were careful to dispose of our empties in the bin. Then we went back to singing "Day by Day" at full volume.

The tours were a rare experience for me. On tour I was surrounded by people I seemed to belong with. They didn't all like me, but at least they didn't all hate me. I could talk, laugh, and joke in this company. The choir and the tours in particular were the only times this happened.

We visited many other wonderful places on tour, including Oban on the west coast of Scotland. From there we went on to sing in the tranquil abbey on the island of Iona, in the Inner Hebrides. With its white sands, Iona was like a Caribbean desert island, if it weren't for the brisk cold April wind. On this trip our pound bought us battered haggis and chips, something I had every night. It was here in Scotland that I first developed a love of taking scenic photographs. There was something special about the land.

The last trip I went on with the choir was to the Lake District. Here we stayed not on floors in sleeping bags, but in the youth hostel in Hawkshead. My passion for hill walking started in earnest here as well as my love of the area. I climbed the Old Man of Coniston in pretty terrible conditions, but I knew how to read a map and the clouds parted on the way up. It was inspiring and tiring all at once. My calves were on fire from walking quickly, but the climb was worth it. The Lake District is one of the most beautiful places on earth, and I have been visiting there for over fifteen years. The stillness of the area, and the views of the lakes and valleys, gave me some peace with myself, and helped me to like my own company.

Being on tour was infectious and good for my soul. We always got plenty of fresh air, and I loved the walks we went on. With my compact 35 mm camera I could capture a moment in time. Not only that, but I could capture a favourite view. That view can be the same place, but on a different day it will always be different. Photography has taught me that perspective changes everything. The same view can change in so many ways—just like life.

I sometimes think that the only reason I survived school was the choir. Not only did it mean I was able to avoid the bullies on Wednesday lunchtimes and Friday evenings, but it gave me a sense of belonging that I didn't have anywhere else. The other children in the choir seemed to put up with me without too many issues, perhaps because they weren't the most popular kids, either. I always found that when I was singing, all my problems melted away and I lost myself in the music. Whenever I sang I was appreciated, except in the assembly hall at school, where even fellow members of the school choir kept quiet when I was picked on.

Overall, I seemed to be welcomed when I sang. It was the only time that I truly believed I belonged. I couldn't put my finger on why I felt this way, but I suspected that if I understood the mystery of how singing made me feel, it would disappear. Singing came naturally to me and was something I didn't have to think about. It was the one good thing that stayed constant in my life at this time. My voice was my friend, and at times I felt as though it was my only one. Singing was the only thing I did that seemed to have universal appeal. The more I sang, the more I wanted to sing professionally. It was my life's dream, but I didn't know how to achieve it, especially when my exam results didn't go my way.

The fifth year at Redcliffe was when academics got serious. As I was in the top stream, this meant I was expected to do mostly GCE (general certificate of education) O-levels. Not all the teachers had complete faith in me, however; although I had improved, I still wasn't putting in the amount of effort they thought I should. As a consequence, I was told that for German I would be sitting the lower-standard CSE (certificate of secondary education) examination, unless I wanted to pay for the O-level examination myself.

I used my newspaper round to pay for the private sitting of the German O-level, as I felt confident that I could prove the teachers wrong. And prove them wrong I did. I passed my O-level German, which left me with a feeling of satisfaction. My other results were mixed: I did well at religious studies and passed both history and English literature; but I sat my English language early and did less well than expected. I also only got a mediocre CSE grade 3 in both mathematics and physics. As I mentioned earlier, at one point I'd considered becoming an artificer, but now an engineering career was not possible: in the UK, certain grades were needed to train for some professions.

My biggest disappointment, however, was my music O-level. I did okay on the basic theory, but struggled a little at the advanced level. For all my love of music, I lacked compositional skills. In fact, my compositions were truly terrible. Not only that, but I was injured when it came to performing them. I'd lost my temper with a boy at school who was hitting me, and thumped him; but I was so unused to actually hitting back that I'd kept my thumb inside my fist and broke my thumb. I am right handed, but could only use my left hand—with predictable results.

In the end, I got an A for performance, recording "The Heavens Are Telling" from *The Creation* by Joseph Haydn. I sang all four parts: soprano, alto, tenor, and bass. My voice had changed, but it hadn't broken in the usual sense. My compositional skills (or rather the lack of them) held me back though, so that my final grade was a lowly E (the lowest grade you could get without failing). I was very disappointed, as was Mr. Weaver. He felt that I could have done better on the theory part of the exam, although he did agree with my view that I wasn't a composer.

I felt at the time that failing my music O-level was a big stumbling block to becoming a professional singer. It meant that I couldn't study music at A-level, and to my naïve eyes, I thought that was the only route to having a singing career. I also worried whether I was cut out to sing professionally, anyway. To open myself up to perform professionally would be to risk criticism, and I wasn't sure how I might take that. I wasn't confident that I was strong enough to put myself in the firing line of such scrutiny. My parents were very supportive, but I never raised with them the idea of singing professionally. I had come to the conclusion that my singing was mine, and mine alone.

I went back to performing at local competitions, gaining success at the Bristol Eisteddfod, and winning the Musical Theatre and Gilbert and Sullivan classes, performing "Maria" from Leonard Bernstein's *West Side Story* and "Free from His Fetters Grim" from *Yeoman of the Guard*. These wins were very satisfying because, as a treble, I had never won a class at Bristol Eisteddfod. Despite that, I was still nervous about criticism, and I dreaded being told I was not good enough at the one thing I thought I was any use at.

Rather than considering it a career option, I decided to continue my singing as a hobby. I didn't think I would ever sing full time as a profession. I wasn't sad or even disappointed with this conclusion. It just felt inevitable. Singing was my private consolation for what I had gone through. I didn't want to share it more than I was comfortable with. It was mine and no one else's. In terms of a vocation, I set my sights on other things.

Although I had only got an E in music, I had done sufficiently well overall to proceed to sixth form. I chose to take the more advanced A-levels in religious studies and history, and the new GCSE (general certificate of secondary education) exam in American studies. Religious studies and history were both very strong subjects for me. For a while I thought about being a vicar again, just like I had at the age of seven. But choosing it just because I could sing as part of the job wasn't the right motivation. Being a vicar was a vocation, not a job, and so I ruled this out.

All my subjects required plenty of reading, which suited me down to the ground. On top of which, there were only two of us in the religious studies class in my year, so we got very good one-on-one attention. The standard of my work was generally quite high, especially in the first year. I found the study of American history and culture fascinating, including studying the Amish, looking at the root causes of the War of Independence, and how the Boston Tea Party had been an important precursor for the troubles ahead.

I did well in the end-of-year mock A-level exams, gaining two C's. Now came the time to think about my university choices. I chose Newcastle, Nottingham, and Exeter universities as my three preferred places, and while Exeter declined me, I got interviews at Nottingham and Newcastle and gained offers from both. I would need to perform at my best to gain the place I wanted.

Unfortunately, the disorganization that had dogged my school career caught up with me like it had before. I started to trail behind with work and do more and more of it last minute. Part of that was because I was doing some Gilbert and Sullivan singing with a company called Bristol Catholic Players in Northern Bristol, and this was taking up more and more of my time. I had been introduced to the company by someone in church. I was only in the chorus, but I was often asked to substitute for soloists. As my A-levels approached, my first production was looming in front of me. The more I sang, the more my grades diminished.

This did not please certain people in the school, and my situation wasn't helped by the fact that I had taken on a part-time job as a shelf stacker in Waitrose, which ate up yet more of my time. The teacher responsible for exams put me under pressure to ensure that I was doing sufficient work, but I got support from my subject teachers. They were used to how I worked, and were still confident that I could achieve my target grades if I applied myself a little better.

Everything changed, however, on the opening night of *HMS Pinafore*.

It happened on my way up to Westbury Park for the performance. I had taken one bus to Eastville Tesco and needed to get another bus from there to Henleaze; from there I could walk to Newmann Hall, the performance venue. Seeing my next bus on the opposite side of the road, I crossed rather clumsily in front of the bus I had just alighted from.

Then everything went black.

I came around to find a crowd surrounding me. Bemused, I tried to get up.

"I have to get to Henleaze," I said weakly. "I have to be on stage at seven thirty."

"You're going nowhere until the ambulance gets here, young man," came a concerned voice.

The person talking to me was the man who had hit me in his car. He was a doctor who lived in Fishponds, and had been about to do his shopping. The way I had crossed the road was pretty careless: I'd had no chance of seeing the car that was coming round the bus. I was taken to Frenchay, a hospital I was very familiar with. On being unloaded from the ambulance, I was asked to produce a urine sample. I hadn't yet had an X-ray, and I hobbled to the patients' toilet and had to run all the taps to try and get myself to wee. It took ages. I must have looked quite a sight in my hospital gown, hobbling around with a partially full plastic urine bottle.

When the results had been examined, I was told that I was to be admitted to ward thirteen. The doctors were concerned about my kidneys, and needed to X-ray me the following day. This they did, but not before injecting a dye into my system that would highlight my kidneys to check for damage. It had a horrible taste and smell, but I wasn't allowed to drink any liquids, which meant that I couldn't get rid of the unpleasant taste. It was revolting, and stayed with me all day.

The news wasn't good. The doctors found that not only were my kidneys badly bruised, but also that I had a hairline fracture to my lower fourth vertebrae. This meant I had to stay in ward thirteen for another week, and that I would have restricted movement for some time after. This was the last news I needed—not only was I meant to be singing, but my A-level exams were only three weeks away.

I didn't yet know the exact date of my exams. I explained the situation to the ward sister, who was kindly if a bit of a battle axe. She said that if my school let them know exactly when the exams were, I could sit the exams in the hospital school, as it was an accredited site. My parents contacted the school, but heard nothing back.

I was discharged for care at home and spent two weeks in a collar and wheelchair. Despite the discomfort, I went to Newmann Hall to watch the Bristol Catholic Players' production of *HMS Pinafore*. I sat in pride of place in the middle of the hall in my wheelchair. The funniest thing was that the hall had a toilet for the disabled, but I parked my wheelchair outside it, got out, and used the ordinary males' toilet. This got a few titters from the regulars at the club.

After the half-term, I visited my family physician, Dr. Cussens. He told me that I should really not be taking my exams in the condition I was in, but agreed to write a letter to the examination board so they could take my condition into account. But then at ten thirty that night, the phone at home rang. It was the head of sixth form.

"Don't bother revising now," she told me, "but you have your first A-level examination at nine tomorrow morning."

I was shocked. I had asked several times for the dates of the exams, but no information was given to me. Worse still, I had asked about sitting all my exams in the main hall so I wouldn't have to climb the stairs to the top floor where my exams were due to take place. Despite my condition, I was told they couldn't guarantee this.

Sure enough, I arrived at the school the following morning and was told that it wasn't possible for me to take any of my exams in the main hall, as all the places were full. I shrugged my shoulders and struggled my way up eight flights of steps to the top floor. I handed in my doctor's note to the examinations teacher, and sat down. Every one of my six exams would be sat on that top floor. There were no lifts, and this meant that I sat every paper in absolute agony. I didn't tell anyone at home about the situation. Every problem I faced in life, I felt I had to solve myself.

I did my best, but I wasn't able to concentrate because of the pain. My doctor was right: I should never have sat the exams. The only successful one was my American studies GCSE, which I got a C in, but much of that was gained through the coursework I had done over the last two years. For the others, I had the ignominy of two unclassified A-levels. I later found out that the examinations teacher had decided not to send in my doctor's note: he felt that I hadn't worked for my A-levels, so I deserved no discretion.

I almost gave up on my A-levels because of how angry I was with the school for its lack of support. Thankfully I did persevere, and successfully retook them the following January, after having interviews for university colleges in Chester, Southampton, and Plymouth. When I applied to the University College of St. Mark and St. John in Plymouth, I was accepted on the condition that I pass my A-levels. When I saw the examinations teacher, he made a point of saying, "You worked for them this time. Well done." I didn't tell him that I had actually handed in *less* work.

I finally had the qualifications to go to university. At this point, my plans were to aim at a career in retail management. With professional singing discounted as a possibility, this seemed a safe, reliable, and very low-risk strategy. The question for me was whether, after all the trials of school, I would be allowed a completely new beginning at university. I certainly hoped so.

PART TWO

Struggles

CHAPTER SIX

Off to University

I'M STILL NOT SURE how we managed to get everything into the car. My parents had hired an estate, or station wagon, for the trip to take me down to university. Even so, with all the boxes of books, clothes, and other belongings, it was still a tight squeeze. With the exception of Jane and John, my whole family was squashed into the car to take me down to Plymouth, eager to see where I would be spending the next three years of my life.

We took the scenic route down from Bristol, avoiding the motorway and sticking to the smaller roads. It was a late September day, and the Devon countryside looked beautiful in the autumn sunshine. As we went round Exeter, and followed the road across the windswept beauty of Dartmoor, I stared out of the window and wondered what university life would be like.

I'd chosen to study philosophy, theology, history, film, and television as part of a BA with honours humanities degree at the College of St. Mark and St. John, known affectionately as Marjons.

Many people at church had argued against my studying philosophy, as they were worried it would cause me to question my faith. My response was that if my faith didn't survive my own questioning, then it wasn't strong enough to survive anything else.

As the hire car pulled into Plymouth, I immediately knew this was a place I would grow to love. Plymouth, like Bristol, is another vibrant southwest city, a hundred-odd miles further south down on the Devon coast. Plymouth is an important English port that has long played its part in history. It was here that Sir Francis Drake was famously told of the arrival of the Spanish Armada in 1588; legend has it that he finished his game of bowls before responding. It was here, too, in 1620, that the Pilgrim Fathers set off for the New World. Like Portsmouth, where I enjoyed so many summer holidays, Plymouth is today an important naval centre: HMNB Devonport in the west of the city is the largest naval base in Western Europe.

I was attracted by the rugged coastline and the historic Barbican area close to the seafront. Yes, it rained a lot, but it was not too far from home and at the same time far enough away for me to feel that I was having a new start. I was happier there than I had been at school. I still struggled a little in meeting people and being in crowds, but there was none of the name calling and bullying I had been subjected to at St. Mary Redcliffe. I made some good friends, the closest of which was a fellow named Phillip. He and his friend Neil would be my housemates in years two and three.

I enjoyed my studies and the challenges, particularly film and television studies and philosophy, but by the end of the first year

I had to drop a subject. We had been studying the Renaissance, and although I enjoyed studying the art and texts such as Machiavelli's *The Prince*, I decided to drop history. It was a tough decision to make as I enjoyed History, but I felt that a new subject, film and television studies, would give me a new direction.

My favourite thing about film and television was that I got to study some of the greatest movies of all time, such as *Double Indemnity*, *The Postman Always Rings Twice*, and *Unforgiven*. I liked the film noir period of the 1930s and 1940s because it had a mood that was easy to identify; there was a darkness about the films, a sinister undertone. But my favourites were from the kitchen-sink drama era of British cinema in the late 1950s and early 1960s. I loved films like *Saturday Night and Sunday Morning* and *Room at the Top*, which were both entertaining and shocking; the films dealt with controversial issues of the time such as abortion and mixed-race relationships. My favourite film of all was Tony Richardson's *Look Back in Anger*; Richard Burton was brilliant, shocking, and nasty all at once. I loved watching and learning about these films, and it rarely felt like work at all.

Philosophy was one of my favourite subjects for a different reason. It was genuinely challenging, yet there was never a right or a wrong answer. We were free to have open debates, and we studied things as varied as the Thatcher years and their relationship to morality, and whether her successor John Major's "classless society" was an achievable aim. I think by far the most difficult book I studied in philosophy was Søren Kierkegaard's *Either/Or*. I'm not sure I ever got my head round that one!

During this time, Saddam Hussein's invasion of Kuwait was about to become all-out war. It was a worrying time because my brother John was on HMS *Gloucester*. The *Gloucester* was to play a major part in the war, taking out an Exocet missile that had been aimed at the British fleet; it was also the ship that would have had to sacrifice itself if the USS *Missouri* was targeted.

As the war started, I was shocked at the jingoistic attitude amongst some of the students; to get extra money they had signed up to be reservists, and now they were scared they would be sent to war. I was concerned for my brother, whom I knew was in harm's way. I was listening to a lot of Chris de Burgh's music at the time, and on a piece of paper I wrote out part of his song "Borderline," which talked about the futility of war, and taped it to my room door. It upset me when someone wrote underneath it that those in the armed forces were meant to lay down their lives for their country. It was a challenging time, but thankfully John returned unscathed three months later.

In the early evenings of my first few months at college, I could often be found waiting for the phone at the porter's lodge. This was before widely available mobile phones, so anyone who wanted to make a call joined the queue for one of the hall of residence's few call boxes. I'd have my phone card with me, something I seemed to be spending a small fortune on at the beginning of college. All of which was because, with my typical sense of timing, I had got into a relationship just before I went to university.

Allison was the daughter of some family friends. She was pretty, funny, fairly outgoing, and had very fair skin and red hair. I'd always had a thing for redheads, and I went out on a limb and asked Allison out on a Sunday after the communion service. I waited by the church while Allison came back from helping her mum at Sunday school.

"Hi," I said, somewhat awkwardly.

"Hi," she replied.

"Fancy watching a film later in the week?"

"Sure," she replied, to my huge relief. "What's showing?"

Allison was only the second girl I had been out with. My first relationship had been with Helen, a girl at Redcliffe school, and we were together for eighteen months. My father didn't approve, and we had a number of arguments about her. When we split up, I didn't tell him, as I didn't want to give him the satisfaction. I thought it was perhaps just because he didn't like Helen, but he had the same attitude toward Allison. We quickly became very close, and this bothered my father as he felt that our relationship might put the families' friendship in jeopardy. This left me feeling that I couldn't win. He also seemed to think that if I met someone, then I would somehow move away from our own family.

One particular date early on became memorable for all the wrong reasons: I was due to see Alli at the Golden Lion pub on Frenchay Common, and cycled into the centre of Bristol beforehand as I needed get a few odds and ends. I cycled down the main cycle route that ran on a disused railway. I got to the Lawrence Hill area, and was making good speed, when suddenly I was on the ground: I had collided head-on with a mountain bike.

The other guy's wheel was buckled but apart from that, unharmed. My bike, however, was a mangled mess, the frame completely twisted by the impact. I was rubbing off the dirt from my grazed hands when one of the people who had come over to help told me to look at my leg.

Blood was coming through my trouser leg. I pulled it up and was shocked by what I saw, because I had not felt any pain at all. In coming off the bike, I had landed on the pedals, which were made from sharp, jagged metal. I was looking at a gaping hole in my knee.

An ambulance was called and along with what remained of my bike, I was transported to Bristol Royal Infirmary. As I waited there, a doctor came in and had a look. I've never been squeamish, so the blood didn't bother me. The doctor got me to bend my knee and flex it again.

"Well, there's one consolation," she said with a sigh.

"What's that?" I asked.

"You won't need to get into a queue for X-ray."

Her words started to make sense when, after giving me seven injections of local anaesthetic into the area round my knee, she put her whole hand *into* my knee and started to feel around.

"No broken bones," she concluded, "but you've cut your tendons and ligaments in half."

It took thirty-five stitches inside my knee that would later dissolve, and twenty stitches on the outside that would need to be removed when the wound healed. I wanted to see Alli, and despite the anaesthetic wearing off, I stupidly walked the three miles to Frenchay to meet her and her friends. That night, I didn't sleep because of my exertions. My leg was in agony, and would take over a year to heal properly.

When I left to go to university, I found it difficult leaving Alli behind. She came down with me when I moved into the residence halls, and it was incredibly hard to say goodbye. We remained in the hallway for ages; I held on to Alli for as long as I could.

"Call me later," Alli said.

"But I don't want you to go," I said.

"I know," said Alli, touching my cheek. "It won't be long before you're in my arms again, honest."

Reluctantly I let her go. My room felt bare and empty.

I had a tendency to hold on too hard to someone I cared for, and to fall in love too hard, too quickly. I so desperately wanted to love and to be loved back. Being apart, therefore, brought pressure into our relationship.

I couldn't afford to go up to Bristol very often, so I spent lots of time corresponding with Alli by letter; we would regularly sign off with a quotation from a song. We also exchanged mix tapes. And whenever I could, I spoke to Alli at night, waiting my turn for the public phone to be free, phone card in hand.

One time, I managed to use our phone conversations to surprise her. I was still having dental treatment at Bristol Dental Hospital, and one particular week I was back home but hadn't told Alli I was there. I walked to the phone box round the corner from her house and gave her a call. I didn't let on where I was, and we talked normally for about ten minutes.

"You know what I've gone and done?" I said. "I wanted to read you an excerpt from a song, but I've left it in my room. Can you wait on the line a minute, and I'll go and get it for you?"

I knew that the phone in Alli's house was right by her front door. So while Alli waited, I walked quickly round the corner and gave it a knock. When Alli saw me, she almost jumped through the ceiling! I got one of the longest kisses ever from her.

Back in Plymouth, I found being apart from Alli difficult to deal with. I hated being away from her, and the demons inside constantly asked me why someone like her would be with me. All I could see was all the mistreatment I'd had at school and from Mr. Burton-Barri, which convinced me that I was still worth nothing. I hadn't told Alli what I'd been through. She knew about the bullying as we had attended the same school, but she knew nothing about the abuse. I couldn't tell her, fearing she would see how worthless I really was.

The more I thought about it, the more I felt that sooner or later Alli would find someone better. It got to the point where I didn't want Alli to go to a party in case she met someone else. Just a little bit of harmless flirting would be enough to set off my insecurity, which came across as jealousy and possessiveness.

Being apart and having these demons to deal with meant that our relationship was doomed. I was back in Bristol as I had a lecture-free reading week, when Alli gave me a letter explaining that she wanted us to be only friends. I took it badly. I didn't want to accept it, and tried to discuss the situation with her. I was quite pathetic and even threatened to do away with myself. This upset her, and was possibly the most unpleasant thing I'd ever done. It didn't make any difference, and a week later Alli started going out with the person I had always seen as my rival for her love. I didn't blame her for that; I realized I had driven her to it.

I returned to university after that reading week absolutely devastated. I had the cuddly monkey Allison had given me at the start of the university year for me to imagine it was her while we were apart. As the coach made its way to Plymouth on a grey, wet early Monday morning, I held it close and cried. I felt quite alone.

* * *

One of the most important parts of university is the social life. For me this was still difficult, as I didn't want to get too over-drawn at the bank, and I still didn't have a clue how to handle myself in large groups. But after my relationship with Alli had ended, I made an effort to get involved in all sorts of activities.

On Thursday nights, I went to the Union Street area of Plymouth. This was student night, so beer was cheap and the club's admission was free. I was (and still am) hopeless at dancing. I didn't have the confidence to just get up and not care how I looked. So I only danced to music like Dexy's Midnight Runners' "Come On Eileen," "Happy Hour" by the Housemartins, and "Love Shack" by the B-52's. The reason for this was that in these songs, the "dancing" was basically just flailing your arms and legs about, so it didn't matter how terrible you were!

Occasionally some of the girls at uni would feel sorry for me and ask me to sit with them, but I had no idea how to ask them out. They always looked so good moving to the early-nineties techno music, whereas I found it impossible to dance to. That didn't help my confidence. Alli was no longer around, but I was unable to pluck up the courage to find a replacement.

Away from the club night, I threw myself into music and sport, although I was still struggling with the injuries from my bike accident in Bristol. I tried unsuccessfully to start running again, but found that my knee would seize up in no time at all. I turned to swimming, which was easier, but it bored me rigid. In the end, I started playing basketball.

That might sound strange—a five-foot-seven basketball player with a dodgy knee—but it's true! I played for the mixed basketball team for Marjons and was quite successful, even if for the majority of the first year I hobbled round the court. I never jumped up to the basket to tip the ball in like someone twelve inches taller than me would do, but in spite of my temporary disability I managed to find a way to move round the court, and was pretty good at snatching three-pointers. I got great satisfaction from scoring from very unlikely positions.

Once my knee had healed, I also represented the university at the UK student cross-country championship in Sunderland. I had always been successful as a runner in my teens. I used to run for Bristol Athletics Club in the Gloucester and Gwent Cross Country Leagues, and also represented my county. So I was keen to show what I could do.

My knee had only just healed properly by the time of the championships in January 1992. On the way up to the northeast, we got stuck in heavy snow in Richmond, North Yorkshire, and had to push our minibus for over a mile through the snow, which did my knee no favours at all. As a result, I had a very poor race the following day, only just managing to finish, and that was the very last time I ran a cross-country race. I was disillusioned and disappointed. It wasn't the end of my running and certainly not the end of activity, but it was the end of my days as a competitive athlete.

Towards the end of the summer term of 1992, I took part in a long-distance walk that started in Manchester. It was called the Bogle Stroll, named after a local ghost. "Stroll" was a bit misleading: it was sixty-three miles walked nonstop in a circular route that started in the centre of Manchester and went through Wigan, Standish, Parbold, and Chorley. We got some abuse as we walked past some of the pubs at closing time, and some participants were even beaten up. There appeared to be no reason for the hostility—our attackers were simply louts who'd had too much to drink. I completed it in just over sixteen hours, having to run the last two miles, as my legs were seizing up and I had to use different muscles to complete the course.

In terms of music at university, there wasn't really much of a choral tradition to speak of; Marjons only had a tiny choir. I became a member of Plymouth Philharmonic Choir, joining them for one of the most challenging choral pieces ever written: William Walton's *Belshazzar's Feast.* This is a brilliant piece of music, full of great drama and wonderful orchestral interludes. We were fortunate to be accompanied for the performance at Plymouth Pavilions by the Bournemouth Symphony Orchestra under the baton of Andrew Litton.

My creative output also encompassed a pantomime held in March 1991. I played the part of a salty sea dog, a young version of Captain Birdseye in the students' interpretation of the fairy tale "Aladdin." There were many dodgy jokes (as is normal in the British pantomime tradition), and I panicked the directors by waiting until the night before the first performance to learn my lines. I didn't miss a single line, though. My parents recorded the performance, and I have since confiscated the VHS tapes— so they are never ever seen by anyone else!

As the end of my third year approached, the mark I got for my dissertation was going to determine what degree I'd come away with: a high grade coupled with good final exams results would give me a 2:1. Getting an upper second meant better job prospects or qualification for a higher degree. The dissertation had to be fifteen thousand words long and handed in, fully bound, at one o'clock on a Monday afternoon. By the Saturday morning before the deadline, I still hadn't written a single word.

I was no different at university than I had been at school. I always did the required reading, but started the work at the last possible moment because that was how I worked best. It was as if I thrived on the sense of urgency, where there was nothing for it but to pour everything into it right up to the wire.

I would do much of my work at night in the days approaching a deadline. At one point in my final year, I had four three-thousand-word essays that had to be in at the same time. I left them all until the last week, which meant I had to work through the nights to get them completed. Every night that week, I went for a four-mile walk to clear my head and then sat down to work. I drank several cups of coffee and had music playing very quietly on a tape deck. It wasn't the caffeine in the coffee that kept me awake, but instead the trips to and from the toilet!

I completed all four essays just on time, with next to no sleep over the period. I handed them in and went to a theology lecture, where I'm told that my snoring was a source of amusement to the class. When I got home and sat in front of the TV, I soon fell asleep again. I woke up two days later with a very sore neck. It was all worth it, though. When I got the essays back, they were the highest marks I'd received in my three years at Marjons, and made getting a 2:1 a real possibility.

My dissertation was in philosophy of religion, under the title "Which Way to Theodicy? A Study of the Solutions to the Problem of Evil and Suffering in a God-Created World." I read widely, and ended up arguing against the original sin doctrine of Saint

Augustine, since I didn't think it fair that people should pay penalties for things their predecessors had done.

The subject was more than just a philosophical issue for me. At times while writing and preparing my dissertation, it left me asking myself, Why me? Why did I have to go through the physical abuse at school? Why did I have to go through the sexual abuse by Burton-Barri? I really struggled to accept the necessity of suffering. Where was the greater good? How was my suffering helping others? How was it meant to help me?

I kept searching for answers, but never found anything satisfactory—just more and more questions. I was torn. Despite my strong arguments against the Augustinian idea of blaming mankind for its suffering, I still blamed myself for the abuse and for my own suffering. Blaming the perpetrators for what I had been through didn't work, as to my mind there had to be a reason why they did what they did. I thought I was the common denominator.

By the Saturday morning before the dissertation was due, I had written up all my notes by hand and was ready to type them up on the university computers over the weekend. As I made my way to the sports block, I passed some workmen outside but thought nothing of it. Once I got to the computer, I'd written about four thousand words when suddenly it went dead. The workmen, it turned out, had drilled through the network cables and everything I'd typed was lost.

Because it was the weekend the library was shut, so I couldn't use the computers there. I went to the porter's lodge and explained the situation.

"I suppose you could use the computers in the history section," the porter offered. "But only until I finish my shift, as I'll have to lock up then."

Immensely grateful, I started typing again. By the time the porter came to lock up on Sunday evening, I was close to completing fifteen thousand words. This left me the next morning to finish the typing, put all the chapters into one file, spellcheck the full document, get it bound, and hand it in.

I got up early on the Monday and made good progress. I was looking good to hand in the work, bang on time. I set about putting the chapters into one document and was just saving it before spellchecking it, when . . .

Blink!

To my horror, there had been another power cut! For the second time in two days, I had lost power as the document was saving. I had lost all my work, which meant I had to retype the whole dissertation from start to finish. I was never going to be able to do that in two hours, so I went to the humanities office and spoke to the staff. I begged for an extension, and was given until ten the following morning to get the dissertation in.

Thankfully, the same porter who'd been helpful before was on a late shift and he again allowed me to use the computers in the history section. This time, I managed to get it all typed out. I just had time to spellcheck the document, but not to grammar check it, before I had it printed and bound. I handed it in just in time.

In my final exams, my luck appeared to have turned: two of the essay questions on my philosophy of religion paper were on areas I had covered in my dissertation. Having written and rewritten my dissertation, I was able to remember many of the sources and quotes to use in arguments. I got first class honours marks for the paper, and when I got my dissertation marks from my dissertation supervisor, I was overjoyed. I had scraped a first class grade for that as well.

Adding in my previous marks, I was right on the border between getting a 2:1 or a 2:2. As a result, my dissertation was called in for external assessment. The external examiner agreed with my dissertation supervisor's grading for the content, but took seven marks off for typographical errors; mistakes I would have picked up if I'd had time to do a grammar check. I was very disappointed, but a 2:2 with honours was still a good degree.

The question now was, what was I going to do next? Having concluded that a professional singing career wasn't possible, my plan while at Marjons was to go into retail management. When I graduated, however, the British economy was not in great shape. In 1993, it was just coming out of recession, and although they were just beginning to fall, unemployment levels were still extremely high. Jobs were scarce, and every graduate opening was heavily oversubscribed.

At the end of my degree, I was £1500 overdrawn and under pressure from my bank to repay it. I returned to the temping agency I'd worked for during the holidays and ending up doing a string of manual jobs. I worked in a dairy and then a food factory in Ashton Gate. I was then moved to a company called Bristol Bending Services, which made car parts for Honda and Rover. It was hard and dirty work; I was put on the lathes, and would be black with dirt by the end of the day. Mum and Dad were disappointed that I couldn't find a job more suited to my qualifications, but were proud that I wasn't content just to mope around on benefit.

With no permanent jobs opening up, I decided to continue my studies. I was accepted onto the master's degree in applied theology at Marjons, for which I would be studying part-time, travelling down to Plymouth once a week. With work for the temping agency proving inconsistent, the main issue for me was financing the course.

Help came from an unexpected source. Around this time, I represented All Saints Church at a Deanery conference, which was led by the resident theologian canon of Bristol Cathedral. I had a chat with the canon afterwards, and learned that the cathedral was looking for a temporary verger up until Christmas. He very kindly said he would recommend me for it, and after a short interview I was accepted for the job.

The verger role was mainly a ceremonial one: leading the choir in and out of the cathedral. It was great for me, as it meant I was able to sing every day I was in work! The cathedral was a very special place to sing, with its ten-second echo (it has a very long, high vaulted nave, which means the sound takes a long time to travel to the back of the church). This meant that leading the choir in from the back of the church, we were only just hearing the start of the processional hymn when the organ was already halfway through the verse! We would play catch-up all through the hymn.

At the end of my tenure at the cathedral, I got a similar job at St. Mary Redcliffe Church, where I had spent much of my youth in the school religious services. There was more manual work required here, especially after windy days when I would have to sweep the churchyard. It was a very satisfying experience working in these fine buildings. I have always sat in wonder at how hundreds of years ago, people were able to build such huge and beautiful buildings with their hands, using only wooden scaffolding and pulleys.

This job, too, was only temporary. It came to an end in the spring of 1994, and although I came close to a permanent position at Bath Abbey, it wasn't to be. I struggled to find work and started claiming unemployment benefit—something I hated doing. I continued to apply for lots of jobs, but many of the employers felt I was overqualified.

Although I passed my first year's exam with distinction, I was behind with my term-time work, and my essays weren't of such a high standard. I was also behind with my payments to the university, a situation that got even more difficult when the benefit office threatened to cut off my money if I used it to pay my college fees. This struck me as very strange: I was trying to improve myself and yet they were punishing me for it. I ended up with a county court judgment against my name, and then the college disallowed me from continuing my studies because I had failed to pay the fees. At the time, I was living with my parents and therefore not eligible for housing support, so the money I was receiving on benefit was for my personal use.

My academic career was over, but I did finally find work. In October 1994, I got a temporary six-week contract at the Tesco supermarket chain. It was retail, if not retail management, but that was okay by me. My degree wasn't such that I could simply walk into management, and I was fully prepared to get my hands dirty and work my way up the ladder. As it turned out, I was to spend the next ten years working for Tesco. It was very physical work and I enjoyed interacting with the public. However, often I had to work nights, which was very difficult to adjust to.

As I settled into my new job, I began to take an interest in local politics. My younger brother, as well as Mum and Dad, had already become involved in the Liberal Democrat Party locally, and were helping with leaflet drops. I wanted to be more involved and started to write articles for *Focus*, the local Liberal Democrat newsletter. Since I was used to writing academic papers, my writing style had to change dramatically in order to be effective on a local newsletter. I was told I would need to write as though for a younger reading age, and use a tabloid style.

In 1995, I decided to stand as a candidate for the local elections, since I had become interested in politics and Mum, Dad, and Tony were already involved as well. I had no chance of winning, as the Liberal Democrats had done nothing in the area, Eastville Ward, for a long time. In the run-up to the elections and on election day itself, I helped out in the neighbouring ward to my own, in order to get someone elected there.

I'd had to do canvassing for a few weeks in my first-year holiday, but it wasn't something I'd originally enjoyed. Then I found my own way of doing it: rather than simply asking what party someone intended to vote for, I began by asking if there was anything the local party could do for them. This made canvassing less of a sales routine for me, and was a method I brought into my local area when it was time to start campaigning in my own ward.

In the first elections in 1995, I finished in fourth place, behind a local independent party. I bided my time, and my opportunity came when the sitting councillor resigned her seat. I flung myself into the canvassing, and after a busy campaign I was elected in May 1996, leaping from fourth place to win.

Having both a full-time job with Tesco and being on the council meant that I was very busy. At first, Tesco management was unhappy, as it meant I would take paid time away from the store: company policy was that local community work was given as paid leave. They became more supportive when I interceded between them and a local pub over the return of shopping trolleys the pub had collected because they weren't being picked up in the area.

At twenty-five, I was the youngest person on Bristol City Council. I had a job, and the potential beginnings of a retail career. For the first time in a long while, I felt that my life was stable and that possibilities were ahead of me. But despite all of this, my dreams about wanting to sing would never quite go away.

CHAPTER SEVEN

Unexpected Opportunities

I'LL NEVER FORGET the first time I felt a real buzz from an audience's reaction to my singing.

The moment came during my time at university. Because there had been few singing opportunities in Plymouth, most of my performing was done back in Bristol. I took part in an All Saints Players' production of *Grease*, preceded by a first half of "Songs from the Shows," and it was there that I got this incredible reaction.

The song I'd chosen to sing was "Love Changes Everything" from Andrew Lloyd Webber's musical *Aspects of Love*. I had been listening to it on cassette, and on a whim I bought the sheet music. After two rehearsals with Chris Gammon, the producer for the show and the church's organist, I decided to perform it.

Having listened to my cassette repeatedly, it took me no time at all to sing the song without the lyrics. This allowed me to really "perform," and was perhaps the first time I fell in love with performing. I had always enjoyed singing high notes, and the louder and longer the note was, the better! "Love Changes Everything" was perfect for that; it ends with a high B flat scored for eight beats. On the night of the performance I held it for twelve, and wanted to hold it longer.

I was taken aback by the reaction I got. The response of those listening was overwhelming, and it was the first time I had ever felt the sensation of an audience "buzzing." It was an incredible moment. I loved that feeling. It gave me a shiver down the spine—something I wanted to feel again and again.

Back living in Bristol after university, I started singing in the chorus of Bristol Catholic Players. It was a challenge to find time for everything, what with my job and being a local councillor. I tried very hard to get principal parts in the productions but found myself held back by an unexpected reason: my teeth.

During my time at university, one of my middle teeth had to be removed and the crown on another tooth got damaged. While my singing was said to be sufficiently good, the company considered my teeth to be too much of an issue for me to be given a romantic lead. Of course, I could have had reconstructive dental surgery, like any sensible person might. But I wasn't just some ordinary person. When I encountered an obstacle, I always saw it as something to run away from. I knew that my teeth looked terrible; I would have been stupid not to notice it. But I saw no advantage to changing them.

I'd spent hours and hours in a dental chair before, and that was when it was free of charge at the Bristol Dental Hospital. Now it would involve large financial costs, and I didn't see any way of being able to afford it. I was also stubborn: the fact that

I had been told to my face at an audition that there was no way I would be given a part because of the condition of my teeth angered me. Why should I be dismissed just because of my teeth? It felt unfair.

Since I couldn't get a leading role because of my teeth, I was usually an understudy and sang solos in the concerts we gave in different parts of Bristol. I'd given up on ever getting a romantic lead, a defeatism that on one occasion almost caught me out. I had arrived at Newmann Hall for the performance of *Yeoman of the Guard*, for which I was understudy for one of the minor parts. Understudies are often in a difficult position, as they never get to rehearse the scenes they have to do in case the lead suddenly becomes ill or unavailable. Because I had been told I would never get a main role, I saw no route of progression at all, and didn't see the opportunity of actually doing this minor role as a stepping-stone. All of which meant that I hadn't learned the part. On that night, the person I was understudying didn't show up. I was told to put his costume on, and I was dreading it. With good reason: I sang unprepared, and my confidence was shattered as a result.

Even so, I enjoyed my time in Bristol Catholic Players. Rehearsals were held in the Catholic school by Newmann Hall and conducted by Adrian Anglin, who also played a mean (and I mean *mean!*) Dick Deadeye in the company's production of *HMS Pinafore*. I enjoyed Gilbert and Sullivan because the plays had humour as well as being musically challenging. I also have Bristol Catholic Players to thank for my love of walking, which started with their regular walks on public holidays. One memorable walk was in Gloucestershire on a Boxing Day. Climbing over a stile, I saw a huge puddle and Adrian, the walk leader, offered his hand to assist me. I thought I'd manage by myself, so I politely refused the help. I learned how foolish this was. They say pride comes before a fall, and here this became very true. I misplaced my footing and landed with my face in the mud! It was a lesson learned: sometimes you have to accept help, not struggle by yourself.

"So come on, Paul, who are you going to come as?"

"I thought I might come as an opera singer . . ."

The Horn and Trumpet was a pub in the centre of Bristol next to the Hippodrome, and something of a favourite for the Tesco staff. A group of us played football on Sunday, and we'd go to the pub afterwards for a drink. Sunday night also happened to be karaoke night at the pub. I'd first done karaoke at a local fund-raising night for the Liberal Democrats. It was well received, and so I started singing at the karaoke nights at the Horn and Trumpet.

I would usually sing songs by artists like Elton John and Boyzone. My favourites, though, were songs high in pitch. My top-three karaoke songs were three of the most difficult: Queen's "The Show Must Go On," Foreigner's "I Want to Know What Love Is," and Air Supply's "All Out of Love." The Queen and Foreigner songs I loved simply because they were very high with top D's. "All Out of Love" I liked for a different reason: not only did it go quite high, but the last note I sang was a very long one—over twenty seconds.

One particular Sunday, the hosts announced they would have a competition in the style of a popular TV programme called

Stars in Their Eyes. On the show, each contestant not only sang in the style of their idol, but dressed up to look like them as well. I was keen to take part in the competition; the question was, who should I come as? As chance would have it, I had just bought a music book that contained a few opera arias. It came complete with an orchestral backing track, and one of the pieces seemed perfect, if a bit of a gamble.

"I'm going to come as Pavarotti," I announced to my fellow footballers. "I thought I might have a go at singing 'Nessun Dorma.'"

"What? The one from the World Cup football?" My teammates were impressed, and they raised the stakes a little higher. "Wait until we tell everyone about this at Tesco tomorrow."

Sure enough, word quickly got round Tesco about my "Pavarotti in the Pub" appearance.

"Don't worry, Paul, we'll be there."

"I've got tomatoes I was going to get rid of. Maybe I'll bring those along."

It was quite a step away from my usual risk-averse self. When I announced that I was going to sing, I hadn't even listened to the backing track from the book, never mind actually practised it. I spent the next few days listening to a performance by Pavarotti on the *Three Tenors* cassette tape I had, and then I started to practise. My Italian was terrible; I had sung some Latin in school choir, but I didn't have the first idea about Italian. Thankfully, because the CD had graphics, the words would come up onscreen in the pub just like any other karaoke track.

The evening of the competition came around quickly. To say I felt uneasy would be an understatement. Not only was there the singing, but I had to come up with a costume. I had the tuxedo that I used to wear to Bristol Catholic Players concerts, but by now this was way too big for me. I'd started going to the gym after taking up football and had lost three stone (about forty-two pounds) in less than three months. The tuxedo was now hanging off me, so I had to borrow a couple of cushions and stick them up my shirt to give myself a huge belly.

The next problem was the beard. I went to the joke shop in central Bristol and bought a fake beard. The shop had run out of PVA glue, which is what is used on stage to stick on false beards, so I had to use what I could get hold of. The glue stick I used might have been great for gluing photos and cuttings into a scrap-book, but it was hopeless at sticking a false beard to a face.

That night the pub was full of colleagues from Tesco, and they hadn't come empty-handed. As I took to the stage, I could see *bagfuls* of tomatoes at hand, ready to pelt me if I was rubbish. As I started to sing, I could feel my beard beginning to slip down my chin, and by the end of the performance most of it had ended up on the floor. The singing aspect of my performance, thank-fully, was far more successful. To my relief, the rotten tomatoes stayed in their bags: my co-workers were shocked and surprised that I could sing. I didn't end up winning the competition—it was judged on singing *and* costume—but that didn't matter. I had found my calling.

That joy was to be tempered with shock over the coming two weeks. The next day, I was due to start jury service. I had done jury service once before, while I was a verger at St. Mary Red-cliffe Church. I'd found it a fascinating experience, although I had hoped to serve on a more interesting case than the road rage incident we got, and which failed to have any convincing evidence.

How I was to regret wanting to have a more "interesting" case. I had spent a day or two waiting to be called, when I and fourteen others were ushered into the courtroom. I was one of twelve chosen in what was to be a tough case for me to deal with: the sexual abuse of an eleven-year-old girl by her father.

The girl was now thirteen, and because her father had pleaded not guilty, she was forced to give evidence against him. That she gave her evidence via video link made it an even more harrowing experience. The interview from the prosecuting barrister was kindly, but still all too revealing, with graphic detail of the abuse she had endured—abuse from someone who should have had nothing but love for her.

It angered me when the defence barrister started to question her on behalf of the girl's father. To me it seemed as if the daughter was on trial, not the accused. The defence barrister tried to suggest she had invented what had happened. If she told the court she had made up the whole thing, the barrister promised she wouldn't be in any trouble. His tone wasn't unkind, but you could sense the determination with which he wanted to have his client acquitted. His constant suggestions that she had been lying made me feel uncomfortable.

I could see that the daughter was telling the truth. I recognized the signs. I could tell by how withdrawn she was, and by the pain in her eyes. There was no way that she was telling lies, and there was no way that what her father was accused of could have been an innocent misunderstanding. He had made her perform a sex act on him; it was not a case of a disputed kiss.

I found myself in a difficult position. I *knew* she was telling the truth, but I couldn't tell my fellow jurors why I knew it. Watching that slight little girl bravely give her testimony made me feel like a coward and a weakling. I had never reported the abuse by Burton-Barri, and I could see more reasons to never go to the police. Seeing how strong she had been in the face of the accusation of lying by the defence barrister, I was unsure I would have been the same.

The judge told the jury that in the absence of physical evidence, the case would come down to whom we believed the most. The girl's bravery in taking the stand and speaking about what she had been through had impressed me. The whole jury unanimously found him guilty. There was satisfaction that we had put away the bad guy, but I didn't feel empowered. I knew I wouldn't have had the courage to do what she had done.

As difficult as the case had been, nothing was to prepare me for what happened next. With my jury service not yet over, I returned to Bristol Crown Court the following week and waited to find out when I would be called again. As it could be quite a long time before a decision was made, jurors were encouraged to bring with them something to read or listen to. On Tuesday, I finished the book I brought to read and picked up a discarded copy of the *Bristol Evening Post*.

As I leafed through it, my heart skipped a beat. Accompanying one news article was the photo of someone I could never forget: Victor Burton-Barri, the Sea Cadet leader who had abused me ten years before. As I read the article, it became clear that I wasn't his only target. Burton-Barri had pleaded guilty to thirty-three charges of indecent assault and obscene images and three charges of indecency with children, and was now in prison. The report stated that he had been jailed for his offences, for a total of fourteen and a half years.

I tried to take this information in. I should have felt relieved: Burton-Barri had been locked up and couldn't abuse any more children. Instead, I felt the opposite. As with the sex abuse case I'd been a juror on, I felt like a fraud; like a coward. The other victims had come forward and been able to tell their story. I had simply absorbed it inside myself, perhaps never to tell what had happened. I had done what I had always done when faced with a problem I felt I couldn't cope with: I had run away. I had told myself that if I didn't admit it had happened, then it really hadn't.

I didn't just feel powerless and weak; I also felt the firm vice-like feeling of guilt. It had been twelve years since the abuse from Burton-Barri started. What had I said to him? Nothing. What had I said to anyone else? Again, nothing. I had passed him on the street in Fishponds some years before. Had I pointed the finger at my abuser? No! I had gone on pretending it had never happened, because admitting it would be like admitting I was worthless.

The "what ifs?" started in my mind. How many other children had he abused after me? If I'd had the courage to come forward, how many other children would have been spared abuse at his hands? I blamed myself, not just for allowing him to touch me, and not just for being unable to defend myself. Through my own inadequacies, I had enabled him to abuse countless other children.

It was my fault. I'd known it all this time, and yet I had remained silent. It was in the past, so I couldn't change it. God knows, at that stage in my life I had wanted to scream "STOP IT!" To report it and see him punished for what he had done to me, and to stop him from going on to abuse other children.

I remembered that poor girl in court having to take the cross-examination from the defence barrister. How would *I* have coped with that? Would I have wilted? I didn't know. All I could be sure of was that because I was a coward, other children would forever be blighted by abuse that could have been avoided. I feel that guilt even today, although now that I'm older I realize that I was his victim, and like many victims, I was simply too terrified to come forward.

There was one silver lining to the dark cloud I had been under during jury service: the ITV quiz show *My Kind of Music* was doing local auditions for singers. I had missed the Bristol date due to jury service, but when my service ended a day early, I had another chance: I could use my unexpected day off to go up to London and take part in the next audition.

My Kind of Music was a mixture of game show and singing competition. I had been uncertain about applying, but some of the other karaoke singers at the Horn and Trumpet encouraged me to audition. After much pushing, they got an application form and made me fill it in. They then sent it off on my behalf, to stop me from "not getting round" to posting it.

On a dull, dank day, I got on the National Express bus bound for London and headed down to the auditions, which took place in a Brixton dance studio. There was a pianist there, and a panel of three to sing in front of. I performed "Nessun Dorma" again, using the same backing-track CD I had used in the Horn and

Trumpet (although this time I left the false beard at home). The panel's response was difficult to gauge, and I started the long journey back to Bristol with no idea whether or not I had been successful.

A few days later, however, I got a letter saying I had been selected to perform at the next level. This time it wouldn't be in a private room in front of a handful of people: the next audition was to be held in public, in a shopping mall: Merry Hill Shopping Centre in Dudley, in the West Midlands. To add to the tension, the TV company would be filming the auditions, with only a select few going on to the final stages of the competition.

Being typically last minute, I still hadn't memorised the words to "Nessun Dorma." As my audition time crept closer, it dawned on me that I was going to look an idiot standing up there with a book in my hand. Sometimes at karaoke I'd bring my own tracks with me, so I was used to singing without the words coming up on the screen. Usually I listened to the sample vocal supplied with the backing track. I would listen to the track repeatedly, and then the words would embed themselves in my mind.

In the familiar surroundings of the Horn and Trumpet, the method was fine. But this was completely different. The shopping mall was packed with thousands of people, and there were cameras all round to catch any mistakes. A researcher came over and told me I needed to make my way to the sound desk in the next ten minutes. That was all the time I had to learn the words!

As I made my way to the stage, it wasn't just the audience I was nervous of, but also the host of the show. Michael Barrymore was one of the hottest properties on British TV at the time. He was incredibly tall, towering over me as I took my place, and had great charisma. He'd enjoyed a string of successful TV shows, a well-known catchphrase in the form of "Awright?" and held audiences in the palm of his hand. He was also well known for being unpredictable. As I was waiting my turn, I watched him trying to distract the other contestants, much to the delight of the audience.

I didn't have to wait long to find out what he had in store for me. The very short introduction to "Nessun Dorma" didn't give me much time to settle, and as I sang (in very bad Italian indeed), Michael grabbed a baby from a mother standing close by.

"Do you mind?" he shouted at me, to huge laughter. "You've woken the baby!"

I did my best to keep my composure. Thankfully, Michael didn't disturb me at all after that. I got to the end of the song and was met with a great reaction from both the audience and Michael.

"That was incredible, Paul," he said. "I'm sure we're going to hear more from you."

To my delight, I was selected for the final stages of the competition, which took place in a TV studio in London. The setup of the show was that each singer teamed up with a friend or colleague. Each duo answered quiz questions and demonstrated songs for the other to guess. I thought carefully about my choice of partner, and asked Steve Lenton, the brother of a work colleague. He was very successful in local quizzes and had appeared on one or two TV shows before. Steve was clever, quiet, and very easy to like. We spent the evening before the recording testing each other on quiz questions.

It would be some time before the show was broadcast in the spring of 1999. When I performed "Nessun Dorma," Michael Barrymore was amazed by the power coming from my small body; at the time I weighed under ten stone (about a hundred fifty pounds).

"Can you believe THAT came from that little body?" he said to the audience. "Incredible!"

I was reasonably happy with my singing, although I was acutely aware that I didn't understand the language I was singing in. The show itself only gave me a limited amount of attention. In fact, in its review of the show, the *Daily Mirror* got me mixed up with my quiz show partner. They described "Steve Lenton's" performance of "Nessun Dorma" as amazing!

The lack of fame didn't bother me; that wasn't why I went for it. It wasn't really a talent show as such, but a quiz show with singers. Here, Steve and I complemented each other well. To our amazement, a few of the questions we had tested each other on actually came up during the quiz. This included the final question in the jackpot round.

"Who wrote the song 'Lady'?" Michael asked.

Steve and I looked at each other. We knew it was Lionel Richie, even though Kenny Rogers had sung it first and made it famous. To our delight, and to cheers from the audience, we won £16,000 between us.

There was quite a discussion at work about how the money should be split. Many of my Tesco colleagues felt I should take two-thirds, as we wouldn't have made it on the show at all without my singing. I was adamant, however. We were a team, and therefore we would split it equally. I knew exactly what I wanted to spend my share on. I wanted to start taking singing lessons and also do something about my teeth.

My luck, it seemed, was beginning to turn.

CHAPTER EIGHT

Singing Abroad

WITH MY WINNINGS from the TV show, I started having singing lessons once a week. I got myself a bike, as my lessons were in Bath, at Bath Spa University on the edge of the city. My teacher was Ian Comboy, a former principal bass with English National Opera and various other international opera companies. I immediately got on well with Ian, who told me that I had an innate ability to take onboard what I was told. He was not only a good teacher, but also a great source of advice about my singing career. Ian was someone who appeared to admire my determination to succeed. He had sung with all the major opera companies in the UK, and encouraged me to have confidence in my voice, telling me that I was an extremely quick learner.

Being on national television didn't open a huge amount of doors, although I did perform "Nessun Dorma" at a few expenses-only gigs. The biggest opportunity I received was from a promoter in Kent. He was putting on a show with the Royal Philharmonic

Concert Orchestra to raise money for the cancer care ward at Margate's Queen Elizabeth The Queen Mother Hospital. It was to be a huge occasion, and I was warned that up to fifteen thousand people would be there. Ian told me this would be a good chance for a breakthrough, and over the coming months we worked toward the concert.

At the same time as starting the singing lessons, I had also auditioned for the Bath Opera. The auditions resulted in my getting two smaller parts in *Turandot*: Prince of Persia and Herald. This meant that while I didn't sing "Nessun Dorma," I would be singing its introduction section. It also meant that I would get extremely fit: I was now cycling between home in Bristol and Bath a few times each week, and Bath is anything but flat. It is one of the most beautiful cities in Great Britain, with stunning architecture and historic Roman baths. The city is built in such a way that no matter what part of Bath you are in, to get out of it you have to climb a hill. The one I climbed the most was very steep.

The Bath Opera performances were held at Bath University's main campus; as well as being great performers, many of the cast also became great friends. The musical director would later play the organ at my wedding, and Judy, who played Aida, would sing at the wedding. Again, I'd found myself in a community of like-minded people, and this helped me feel included.

I had my first experience of making a music video when Bath Opera let the local media know I was involved in the production. I ended up walking round the Tesco store where I worked in my uniform, singing "Nessun Dorma" for BBC West's evening news magazine, *Points West*. It was bizarre walking round the store singing, with everyone turning round to look at me.

STRUGGLES

It should have been good publicity for Bath Opera's show that week. But the opera company's publicity team didn't account for the pettiness of local party politics. A short preview was run ten minutes before the feature was due to be shown. In those ten minutes, someone from the Labour Party phoned up and complained that the Liberal Democrats were getting an unfair advantage because of the piece, just before the city council elections. The piece was pulled and only shown some months later, after the election. It meant that Bath Opera lost the publicity opportunity for our performance of *Turandot*.

A few months later, the charity concert in Margate took place. I knew it was a fantastic opportunity, and it was also by far the largest audience I had ever performed for. I had practised hard with Ian, but I was beginning to feel the pressure. The concert was held at Quex Park on the outskirts of Margate, and I knew it from having sung there on a choir tour when I was back in school. Fifteen years later, the park was more rundown than when I'd last visited. The fairground was gone, and it was quite sad to see it in such a dilapidated state.

It was a warm, sunny summer's day, and I was met by the promoter, a nice guy called Albie Park. Albie walked me to the rehearsal area and told me how he had enjoyed my performance on TV.

"You are going to be very successful, I can tell," he said. "Can you promise me that when you make it big, you'll come back to perform for us again, and help us raise more funds for the cancer care unit?"

I was bemused by any suggestion of my making it big in the way he was suggesting.

"Of course," I replied, a little taken aback.

In spite of the television show, I knew that I still was a beginner in this field, and couldn't imagine where my singing could take me. I could dream about it, sure, but I never saw it as being reality.

When the time came for my performance, I felt incredibly nervous. The rehearsal had gone well, although it was a very strange feeling for me to have a large orchestra playing under me. The conductor told me that I would need to follow him, as there would be no way for the full orchestra to follow me; without any formal training, this was all quite new to me.

I needn't have worried. The actual performance went down really well. For the first time I had autograph hunters after a performance! Because my performance was towards the start of the concert, I was able to join my parents and Tony in the audience to watch the remainder of it. One highlight was a piece called *633 Squadron*, which included a real World War II Spitfire flying past. The concert ended with Tchaikovsky's *1812 Overture*, complete with spectacular fireworks.

I felt satisfied with how I'd performed. I could hear the fantastic sounds of the orchestra, and I was thrilled to have been part of that. I enjoyed both having a huge orchestra accompany me and the appreciation of the audience afterwards. I tried not to get carried away with that feeling for fear of coming down with a bump.

I wanted to take my singing to the next level, but part of me wondered whether or not I was ready for it. I was saving up money on top of my quiz show winnings to do something more constructive with my voice, although I didn't know exactly what. Not having gone to music college, I wasn't sure what the next step was.

What I thought was the answer appeared in a monthly magazine called *Opera*. I read about a competition and weeklong course in Barcelona in January 2000. It sounded like just what I was looking for. I raised it with Ian, but he thought it was a bit soon for me to do this. Even so, I decided to take a leap of faith: I felt I had already given a lot to my singing, cycling the thirty-mile round trip three times a week. It was time to test myself.

I flew out to Barcelona on the first of January. There had been lots of scare stories about the "millennium bug," with rumours doing the rounds that planes would fall from the sky, but thankfully these turned out to be false alarms. I stayed at a very basic hotel on Las Ramblas, directly opposite the famous Gran Teatre del Liceu, and took an instant liking to Barcelona. Staying on Las Ramblas was noisy, especially at night, but that didn't bother me. I enjoyed walking round the lanes of the Barri Gòtic and by the sea. I also climbed the towers of La Sagrada Familia church, and took a trip to Parc Güell.

Since then, I've had the pleasure of visiting Barcelona many times; it is a fascinating and beautiful city which continues to delight me. The busy, tree-lined Las Ramblas and the narrow back streets are unique, and the warmth of the Latin spirit is infectious.

On this occasion, however, I wasn't there to sightsee, and before long the lessons started. The first week was to be a short course with the renowned opera singer Magda Olivero, who was ninety at the time. (Today she is alive and going strong at a hundred and three!) I found her to be a very strong person; she had many issues with my voice, and told me exactly what she thought. But she told me in a language I didn't understand: Italian.

"*Fiato!*" she shouted at me, time and again. "*Fiato! Fiato!*"

This meant "breath," and she explained that she thought mine needed more support. I was singing from the throat without using proper breath control. Initially I found the lessons tough, especially as the *répétiteur*, who helped me learn the part, was initially as firm towards me. He softened as the week progressed, and pleaded on my behalf for me to be selected for the course's end-of-week concert. Magda, however, was clear: she felt I had made very good progress, but still hadn't reached the required standard.

While not selected to perform, I enjoyed watching the other singers perform. I had felt in my element as a singer that week. It was a great feeling, even if I had taken a few lumps along the way. I'd also had a good time with the other singers. I was singing every day and getting along with my peers, all of which was a rewarding experience for me.

It was now time to prepare for the competition. I had sessions with my accompanist to go through my initial pieces, "Schlafendes Jesuskind" by Hugo Wolf and "Nessun Dorma." After our rehearsal, the pianist looked at me and said the same as Michael Barrymore had on *My Kind of Music*: it shouldn't be possible for that amount of sound to come out of a slight frame like mine. I took that as a compliment, and entered the competition full of confidence.

The preliminary rounds were held in a large auditorium on Carrer Aragò in central Barcelona. Dad had flown out to watch.

Mum couldn't get the time off work, so she was unable to join him. I was the only British singer taking part in the competition, and it felt like a huge honour to be representing my country. When the time came for my performance, I was feeling very nervous—a lot was resting on my head as the only British competitor.

Although I felt that I had no chance of making the later rounds, I could feel the eager anticipation of the other participants. In the hotel next to the Liceu, the Oriente, the list of those who would make it to the next round was late being announced. Several of us anxiously paced up and down. Sadly, my name wasn't on the list. This wasn't unexpected, but even so, I couldn't help feeling a little disappointed.

Worse was to follow. We were given the opportunity to see one of the judges for detailed feedback, and I decided to take up the offer. I went to a hotel to see the chair of the judging panel, Joan Matabosch, who was the artistic director of the Liceu Theatre. Mr. Matabosch was someone who did not mince his words.

"Your choice of material is wholly inappropriate," he began. "Completely wrong for someone at this stage of your career."

Whilst I was taking that in, his critique continued. "To be honest, I'm not even sure whether you have a voice or not."

I was completely taken aback. While I had expected not to progress, I'd felt sure that the jury would like my singing and hear the potential I felt I had. It was quite uncharacteristic for me to be so confident about something, and this confidence had just taken a severe beating.

I thanked Mr. Matabosch and walked away from the hotel in

shock. Dad, who had been waiting outside, asked me what feed-back I'd been given.

"That man is talking nonsense," Dad said when I told him. "What does he know from just watching you once? You can sing. It's your life, and I'm going to be with you every step of the way."

I wasn't so sure.

"Dad," I replied, "he's artistic director for one of the most important opera houses in the world. Of course he knows what he's talking about!"

I didn't want to debate the issue with my father. I wanted to be alone for a while, and told him so. I walked away from him saying I would be back down when I felt ready. It was to be some time. I went up to my room and cried my eyes out for what seemed like an eternity. Nothing in my whole life had hurt as much as this. I wanted so much for my singing to be a success, and it felt as if I was a failure at this, too.

After a couple of hours, I went down and joined my father for some lunch. The hurt hadn't gone, but I had come to a realization: Ian Comboy had been right. I wasn't ready for this. I had jumped forward too many steps, and my fall had been inevitable.

Despite the setback at Barcelona, I still wanted to improve my singing. I was also very aware that my Italian was nonexistent and needed improving. Not having Internet access at home, I went to an Internet café in the centre of Bristol to see if I could find a suitable course. I wanted something that offered both Italian lessons and also work on my voice.

After a while of searching, I came across something called Italian Lessons for Opera Singers. The course was based in Rimini on the Adriatic coast, and offered twenty hours of Italian lessons a week, as well as some voice coaching. I filled in the online form and hit send.

I couldn't get the holiday time for a complete month off in July, so I was forced to take more drastic action: I took a six-month career break, which meant I was taking unpaid leave. I still had a reasonable amount of the money left over from the quiz show winnings, but not enough to last six months. So once again, I was taking a considerable risk.

I flew out from Heathrow to Bologna on a chilly July day; chilly in Britain, anyway. It was 15 degrees Celsius in London when I left, and I was wrapped up warmly; in Bologna it was well over 30 degrees Celsius, and I had to dive straight into a restroom to change into something cooler.

I still had quite a journey ahead of me, going via airport bus to the city's train station, and then by train on to Rimini. The limited nature of my Italian was quickly apparent. There was an initial scramble for the train, which came in on the wrong platform, something I had been warned about by a barber I knew back in Fishponds. Having run across the tracks with a case and a rucksack, I was relaxing on the train when the guard arrived for the ticket check. He looked at my ticket, gave me an annoyed look, and asked me something in Italian. I didn't understand a word. One of my fellow passengers muttered to the guard:

"Lui è Inglese!" (He's English!)

At this, the guard relaxed, rolled his eyes in understanding, scribbled on my ticket, and handed it back to me. (I hadn't validated the ticket.)

I arrived in Rimini, where I was staying with a family on Via

Santa Maria al Mare, which thankfully wasn't far from the station. I struggled along with a map and my luggage in the heat; it was 35 degrees Celsius by now, and I'd never experienced heat like it. I found the house and rang the bell. I was met with the sound of a dog barking and a woman's voice shouting down from the balcony above.

"*Sì?*"

I muttered a few words: "Uh, *Io sono* . . . I don't know."

"*Che cosa vorebbe?*" (What do you want?)

I didn't know enough Italian to explain myself, so I answered in English. "I'm on the language course *I Malatesta!*"

"*Aspetti!*" she said, signalling for me to wait.

Eventually she answered the door, holding the dog back. It was only a small yappy dog, but from my experience as a paperboy, I knew it was more likely to bite than an Alsatian. She signalled for me to sit and proceeded to make a phone call. She became quite animated, then turned her attention back to me.

She asked me where I came from. I told her that I was from Bristol and I was sorry I didn't speak very much Italian. I wondered whether my rather hopeful estimation of the standard of my Italian had come to bite me on the rear, as she told me in very broken English that she spoke only a little English.

Eventually another lady came; she turned out to be the daughter of the woman I'd been speaking to, and the situation was resolved. I thanked the mother for the cup of tea and headed up to the room that was to be home for the next month.

My Italian lessons started the following morning. Right from the beginning they went well, and I found that I got on with both the teachers and, to my surprise, the other pupils. Those of us on the singing classes quickly developed a real community spirit. There were five of us, and we started to meet up in the evenings and eat out in local restaurants. There was Peter from Denmark, Kylie from Australia, Megan and Angela from New Orleans. Megan and Angela had travelled over together, so they already knew each other. Peter was a very serious individual who appeared to be really intense. Kylie became one of my closest friends.

Along with a few students from the language-only classes, I spent my evenings exploring the restaurants and pizzerias of Rimini, usually round Viale Vespucci, a principal thoroughfare behind the main seafront.

For the first time in my life, I truly felt I belonged somewhere. Not only did I get to sing most days, but I also met up with other people, and they actually liked me. In language lessons, we practised different types of scenarios as we progressed. In one session I came across a question I would have dreaded fifteen years earlier. We were asked to say what we thought of each other. When one of the girls in the class was asked what she thought of me, her response almost made me blush.

"Paolo é bello e simpatico."

This was a new experience for me. Back in school, I'd been used to people saying nasty things to me when asked this, not being told I was handsome and nice.

In the singing lessons we would work on different repertoires with the teacher, Mario Melani. He was the artistic director of the Accademia del Teatro "Città di Cagli," the opera school at Cagli, a small town in the rural part of Marche. I recognised the school from the programs of the Francisco Viñas competition in

Obviously a hairbrush and I were complete strangers when I was seven!

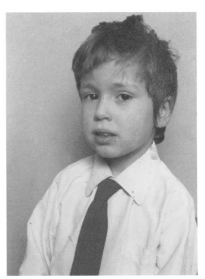

Mum and me with Lady our dog and Jane running towards us.

Me on the deck of HMS *Illustrious* at Navy Days in Portsmouth.

At seventeen I was ridiculously skinny!

Graduation Day.

At Land's End with younger brother Tony after completing an 840 mile walk.

Me with Dad behind me and Tony opposite at a BBQ in Ontario, Canada, 1999.

Oh, for the days when I fitted in a pair of 28-inch waist jeans!

Singing in a church in Ontario, Canada, 2001.

From left; Fulvia, Elisa, and me in Italy.

ur traditional wedding photo outside the church with both sets
parents, plus best man, Mark, standing behind me.

lz and I cutting the cake—I am sure there are times when she'd
ke to use that knife on me!

Julz and me at an awards ceremony in Swansea in 2010.

The performance that changed my life—I had no idea where it would lead.
(Fremantle Media)

Have I really won? Smiling in disbelief after the announcement that I had won in 2007.
(Fremantle Media)

Simon Cowell and I
outside the ITV studios
after my performance
on *Britain's Got Talent* in 2009.
(*Vibica Auld*)

A bit of fun with my
orchestra at the end of my
first UK tour at
Hammersmith Apollo
in February 2008.

Natasha Marsh was great fun
to have on tour with me—
she is a great sport and
a wonderful singer,
London 2008.

The A Team: Julz, me, my manager Vibica, and Jake Duncan, my tour manager, at the UNESCO gala in Dusseldorf, 2009.

On the set of *One Chance*, 2012. Left to right: Julz, Mackenzie Crook, me, James Corden, and Alexandra Roach. (*Liam Daniel* © *2013 The We instein Company. All Rights Reserved.*)

Barcelona that had almost been the nemesis of my career. I got on well with Mario. He was a good teacher; he told me that my main weakness was the amount of tension in my body.

The *répétiteur* for the course was a brilliant pianist called Carlo Pari. He was always great fun, and as well as being a brilliant musician he was a great attraction for the female members of the course with his slightly dishevelled long dark hair. On one occasion, we had a look at a piece from Giordano's *Andrea Chenier*. It was a powerful aria called "Improvviso" in which the main character takes the local lords to task over the fact that they were feasting while the poor struggled to get bread. I was singing one section when I noticed that Carlo had stopped playing because he was laughing so much.

"Be careful with your vowel sounds," explained Lee, one of the assisting teachers who would later become a great friend. "They can change the meaning of the whole sentence."

"If you sing those words on Saturday," a still chuckling Carlo added, "then the audience will laugh at you!"

I was confused. I had sung, or thought I had sung, *"ho un grande pena"* (I have great pain).

"You ended the word *pena* with an 'e' not an 'a,'" Lee explained. "*Pene* means penis. You were singing about how big your penis was!"

At the end of every week, we would perform a concert at different small venues in villages round the local area. The director of the language school, Bruno Fabbri, acted like a local impresario and organised our post-concert dinner. The food was usually quite simple, but always unbelievably fresh and tasty. At this particular meal it was bread, cheese, and cold cuts. I loved the fresh pasta in Italy and also the ever-present smell of garlic and oregano. The wine flowed, followed by the inevitable limoncello and grappa. Both of these were best served ice cold. The limoncello was way too sweet otherwise, and the grappa had a serious kick. The women liked the limoncello but not the grappa, so I ended up drinking nearly all of it!

The first concert was very eventful. We were performing outside the church in Villa Veruchio, not far from Rimini. It was a windy evening, probably due to a thunderstorm in the area. Lee was there to assist Carlo, and it was all she could do to hold the piano's lid up. In the end the weather became too bad and the concert ended early.

We played in a few different places, including Castello di Longiano, but my favourite was one of the capitals of the old northern kingdom of Italy, San Leo. A pretty little town, San Leo is nestled in the mountains surrounding San Marino. Our journey there took us above the altitude where your ears pop, and the scenery was breathtaking.

The month ended all too quickly, and it was nearly time to say goodbye to the rest of the group and head home. But I was approached by Bruno's daughter, Silvia, who asked if I wanted to stay on for a couple more months. I hesitated because I had only set aside enough money for four weeks, and not only would I have to pay the fees but would also have to cover my living expenses. She said she would speak to her father.

Silvia came back and offered me a 75 percent discount on the course fees, although I would have to pay full price for the accommodations. I worked things out and decided I would go ahead. I felt I had made progress, both with my Italian and my singing, and I wanted this to continue.

My stay extended, I visited Florence and Venice with the language school, and was enchanted by both cities. There were more singing sessions, this time with a baritone, Thomas Busch. I returned to San Leo again, and was put in charge of page turning for Carlo.

This was a challenging job. I wanted to sidestep it, as I knew how difficult it would be, trying to concentrate on the music while admiring Carlo's playing on the piano. Page turning is hard enough without its being a very fast-flowing Schubert piece. The piece was sung well by a Northern Irish soprano called Rebekah Coffey, but I couldn't concentrate on her singing because of the speed of the accompaniment. If I was a moment late in turning the page, I got a stern look from Carlo; if I was a moment early, I got a glare.

San Leo was a beautiful city, and its auditorium had great acoustics and atmosphere. The audience tended to be a well-educated one, polite in their applause and a little reserved. This particular Saturday evening was to prove a watermark moment for me. I had already performed Francesco Cilea's "Federico's Lament," one of my favourite pieces, and also Giordano's "Improvviso"—this time with the correct pronunciation of *pena*! I just had one more aria to sing: "Nessun Dorma."

With Carlo at the piano, I tended to perform "Nessun Dorma" more slowly than I had with my backing track. That didn't bother me, because I felt that a few of the popular recordings were too quick, as if in too much of a hurry to get to the famous bit. Unlike my earlier performances, this time, I could sense that something was different: the audience was attentive from the start.

As the piece drew to a close, I remember feeling happy with my performance. Even so, I wasn't expecting the reaction I got from the audience: the whole place erupted. I took my bows and quietly left the stage for the dressing room. Even from there I could hear the audience shouting for me to return. I couldn't believe it.

Carlo came through and told me I needed to perform again. This was completely unprecedented. We discussed what I should perform, as I had already performed everything we'd prepared for the concert. By now, the audience had been applauding for over five minutes and we needed to get back on stage.

I walked out nervously and thanked the audience in Italian. I then announced my next song:

"'E lucevan le stelle,' dall' opera Tosca *di Puccini."*

Again, the audience erupted. I sang the aria and finished to another great reaction. I left the concert on an absolute high. It was the most wonderful feeling in the world, and I didn't want to leave it behind.

My third month in Italy soon came round, and I took lessons from another teacher. This time it was a Russian mezzo-soprano called Svetlana Sidorova. She encouraged me to look at French repertoire by Massenet, and worked me through the famous aria "Pourqoui Me Reveiller." I loved it, and although I didn't agree with everything she said, I made very good progress; and she really helped me get my throat to relax.

She was impressed with my range, and wanted me to work on the junior section of the Rossini Festival in Pesaro. I would need to work hard, and I was really pleased that she felt I had potential. Her approach to stagecraft was to get us moving. She would play Tchaikovsky, in particular *The Nutcracker* and *Sleeping Beauty*. I found this a challenge. She wanted us to move as the music made us move. Her real aim was to make us lose our inhibitions, but that was always going to be a struggle for me.

As my time in Italy was drawing to an end, I had another lesson with Mario Melani. He expressed his amazement at how far I had come in just three months, both in my use of the Italian language and in my singing.

"I'll let you into a secret," he told me. "I was on that panel in Barcelona. I liked your voice then. No one listened to you sing that day. Why? Because your Italian was so poor."

Mario told me that he was so impressed with my progress that he wanted me to join the opera school in Cagli. Not only that, the fee for the year would be the equivalent of £700; he had offered me a special price. I couldn't believe it. This was the same school in which all the semi-finalists at the Viñas competition were awarded a place.

I discussed the opportunity with Carlo and Svetlana. They both felt it was a good opportunity, but there was one very practical problem. How was I to live for the next year? Although the school at Cagli was well respected, the city itself was a small one and lodgings would be difficult to find, not to mention part-time work.

Carlo and Svetlana had another suggestion. The school in Rimini was looking to form its own conservatory. It was to open in January 2001, and jobs would be much easier to find in Rimini. My problem was that I was pretty much out of money. I knew that when I went back to the UK, I would need to return to my job immediately. I had already taken a huge leap of faith coming to Italy for three months. To stay for another year would take more than my confidence and bank balance could account for.

In the end, I put off my decision and headed back to the UK. After all, the I Malatesta conservatory in Rimini would open only five months later. Unfortunately, I was to learn that in Italy many things might be planned with great enthusiasm but that didn't mean they would happen. This was to be the case for the I Malatesta conservatory. Might I have chosen the opera school in Cagli had I not had the cosy option of Rimini? I will never know.

CHAPTER NINE

Looking for Love

WHENEVER I WENT to the Horn and Trumpet for a few drinks, the chat would often turn to the normal discussions young men have. The Horn and Trumpet was a typical British pub of the time: a lively, noisy bar, with a smell of cigarettes that assaulted the senses in the years before the smoking ban. We'd sit there talking, and it never took long for the subject of girls to come up.

It was almost a decade after Allison before I had another girlfriend. Despite having some female friends at university, the relationships never progressed any further, although I did give one very tall blonde a Valentine's card through the university postal system. She told me that she didn't like me "that way." I had heard this many times and just assumed I was unattractive.

The discussions at the pub would get quite raucous, and on one particular Sunday we went round the table asking people when they had lost their virginity. Most of them said at varying times in their teens. I was honest.

"I'm still a virgin!" I said.

The whole bar seemed to go quiet, as if everyone in the pub had heard what I'd said.

"You don't admit to things like that!" one of the group said.

I shrugged my shoulders. I didn't see the point in lying about it; there was nothing to gain. It was just bragging rights. My lack of social skills was showing again, but I genuinely saw no reason to feel ashamed. I was what I was. I'd got by thus far, not measuring myself by other people's standards.

I remained hopeless around girls. From time to time I was approached, but I wasn't able to recognise the signs of a girl liking me, and so I didn't respond in any way, ignoring their advances. If I was given a girl's number by one of the guys in the group, I would just assume they were winding me up. After all, who would be interested in me?

As I reached the end of my twenties, my luck with girls slowly started to change. In between the trips to Barcelona and Rimini, I took part in Bath Spa University's production of Mozart's *Magic Flute*, playing the role of Monostatos.

The performances went well, and my strength surprised two burly rugby players who were to drag me offstage as part of the action. Things got even better for me when it came to the last-night party. I got chatting to a slim, pretty girl named Elizabeth, one of the viola players in the orchestra. She was quite shy, like me, and we hit it off very well. We chatted, and she told me she liked my eyes. We arranged to meet a few days later, and it soon became clear that I would be cycling to Bath even more.

Right from the start my father was unhappy about our relationship, even though he'd never met Liz. I would stay at her place, and we went together to Portsmouth to see my brother John and his then long-term girlfriend. However, our relationship wasn't meant to be, and after a few months we split up. That was fine by Dad; he seemed to think I should be married to my music. In fact, he insisted that it might be better if I stayed single forever, as my singing was more important.

My father and I also differed on other issues. He didn't believe in sex before marriage and expected me to follow his example. Mum always tried to stay out of arguments with Dad, as he tended to be stubborn. I firmly believed that sex belonged within a loving relationship, as an expression of love. My opinion was that a marriage doesn't start with a marriage ceremony. The wedding ceremony is simply the public formalising of the relationship. I was certainly waiting for the right person, but not necessarily for marriage. My father and I disagreed on this, which sometimes led to heated arguments.

It felt as if my father feared that meeting someone would lead me to give up my singing. As much as singing meant to me, I wasn't going to be forced into choosing between that and the love of my life. Like anyone else, I wanted to be loved and held by someone who would accept me for who I was; to be someone's "forever" person. Why should I have to choose between music and love? And as for the singing, it was hard enough just trying to succeed for myself. I didn't want to have to live my father's dreams as well.

When I made the decision to stay on in Rimini, Dad told me he feared I would not return; that I would meet an Italian girl and have a "few bambini." The fact that I had been enjoying my time there must have been obvious, and this wasn't just about the music. I'd made friends with a couple of local Italian girls and I found one of them, Fulvia, attractive. She was pretty, pleasant, and, as I was to discover, extremely perceptive.

I performed one of my favourite duets with Fulvia, "O Soave Fanciulla" from *La Bohème*. During one of our performances at a local spa hotel, we were waiting for our stage time, close to the hotel's swimming pool. Being humorous in a foreign language can be a challenge, but I decided to give it a go. I adapted some of the words from "O Soave Fanciulla," offering my hand and singing to her:

"Dammi'll braccio, mia piscina . . ."

The original word, *piccina*, means "sweetheart"; *piscina* means "swimming pool." To my delight, Fulvia laughed. I could sense that she liked me, but I wasn't sure in what way or how much. My normal cowardly self seized on my uncertainty with the language, and I never made my move. I wanted a relationship with her, but I was worried about how that would work.

In my third month in Italy, Fulvia and I found ourselves being put through our paces. Svetlana, as usual, was trying to make us move and lose our inhibitions. She asked the group to walk round and look into each other's eyes. I found myself face to face with Fulvia. As she looked into my eyes and I into hers, she broke down in tears. I was confused; I'd said nothing. Svetlana stopped the group and we sat in a circle. She asked Fulvia what she had seen.

Fulvia answered in Italian:

"Guardai il suo viso e nei suoi occhi e ho visto la tristezza non ho mai visto prima. Era profondo e non ho potuto andare oltre di esso."

By this point, my Italian was good enough that I understood with a sinking heart what she was saying:

"I looked at his face and into his eyes and saw a sadness that I had never seen before. It was deep, and I could not get past it."

I knew what she had seen. The load I carried was never far away, but I had never been able to talk about it. In that small room, in a language that wasn't my own, I tried to explain what I had been through. I found myself talking to the whole group about the bullying and the abuse. Then both Fulvia and I cried.

Back in Bristol, I came up with a way of getting around my struggles in chatting up women: I started talking with them on the Internet. I saw chatting on the net as a modern way of old-fashioned dating. Online, I was able to be a little less nervous and actually demonstrate a sense of humour. The challenge was always going to come when I met the unsuspecting person.

I got chatting to a couple of women from different parts of the world, including a woman from South Africa. For a while, I chatted with an Australian from Melbourne called Chrissie, but when we met there wasn't the chemistry we were hoping for. I didn't give up, though, and continued to get to know people. Then in January 2001, I started chatting with a twenty-year-old girl from South Wales.

I was working nights at Tesco at the time. I would get home around seven most mornings, have some breakfast, and lounge around in front of the computer doing council casework and chatting on the net. After a few days, there was only one woman I was chatting with: Julz.

It helped me get through the long work night, knowing that I would chat with her before she went to work. After a couple of weeks of this, we exchanged phone numbers and started to talk on the phone. I offered to send a photograph of myself and Julz said that was fine, although she didn't feel comfortable sending one of her own.

We were getting on well, and so we agreed to meet. I still remember the date clearly: 2 February 2001, and the meeting-up point: Swansea Railway Station. Julz had a distinct advantage over me in that she had my photograph, but I still didn't know what she looked like. She could very easily have run away and I would never have known any different. I was thirty, ten years older than Julz, and concerned that she might think the age gap would be a problem.

"I'll be wearing a cream woollen jumper," was all she would tell me.

It was 10:08 a.m. My train from Bristol had just arrived and as I stepped down onto the platform, I saw her: a pretty girl with long blonde hair in a cream-white jumper. The moment I saw Julz, I knew she was going to be special. I was also hugely relieved that she had seen me and hadn't decided to do a runner! We kissed each other lightly on the cheek and discussed what we were going to do for the day.

"How about ten-pin bowling?" Julz suggested.

I agreed. I can be way too competitive sometimes, and it can be a struggle for me to play just for fun, but on this occasion I just about managed it.

After we finished, we went for a short stroll round Swansea. I found myself wanting to hold Julz's hand and wondering how to go about it. What would happen if she said no? If she rejected my hand, then the chances were that I wouldn't try again. I took the plunge and was very relieved when she did in fact hold my hand. We walked onto the seafront and wandered round Mumbles Pier. We sat there together, looking out to sea and eating fish and chips.

Julz and I spent a lot of time together that day, chatting and, yes, kissing and cuddling. It was obvious to me that I had met someone very special, and I wanted to see her again. I was also very aware of my own past and the incident with Fulvia in Rimini. Rather than waiting to tell Julz about what had happened, I told her everything there and then. I knew I was taking a big risk, but in my heart I knew that she was special.

Julz took the information in her stride. I was hugely relieved; I knew that I fell in love very easily, and hadn't wanted the risk of my insecurity ruining things later on. At the end of the date, she dropped me back at Swansea station for my train back to Bristol. I was about to spend some time in the Lake District, and so we agreed to keep in touch via phone and the Internet while I was there. Normally I enjoyed being in the Lake District, but this time all I wanted was to see Julz again.

The first opportunity was the following Sunday. I had been cast in the title role of the Bath Opera production of *Don Carlos*, and although I had a rehearsal in the morning, I would be free from about two in the afternoon. Julz came down to Bath and quickly became a permanent feature at our Sunday morning principal rehearsals. As we got to know each other better, we started to spend the Saturday night together in a hotel and then drive to the rehearsal on the Sunday. It wasn't long before the strains of "O Don Fatale" and other arias were stuck in Julz's head, and she would curse me while she hummed them at work.

The fact that we were spending Saturday nights together meant that I had more arguments with dad. He didn't approve, but I didn't much care. I was falling in love with Julz, and I wanted to spend as much time as I could with her. Dad had two difficulties with the situation: he didn't approve of sex before marriage, and he felt sure that going out with Julz would lead to my giving up singing. The fact that Julz was attending rehearsals seemed completely lost on him. Again, he was suggesting I had to make a choice between singing and love. But I didn't see it that way.

The Don Carlos role was the first lead part I had played, and I enjoyed every minute of it. There was a lot of great music in the opera, and lots of singing for me: an aria plus three huge duets. I was pleased to receive my first critic's review—"high octane passion from Paul Potts in the title role"—and to know that Julz was in the audience, proudly watching on.

Bath Opera had given me the part largely because of the progress I had made in Italy, and I was keen to return to improve further. This time, however, I wouldn't be going on my own. I decided to go for six weeks, again having to take a career break in order to do so, and asked Julz to join me in Rimini for a week, coinciding with her birthday.

Julz had never flown by herself before, and she has never let me forget that for this first solo flight I had booked her on a nondirect flight: she had to fly from Heathrow to Frankfurt and then onwards to Bologna where I would meet her. Unfortunately, the first part of her journey to Frankfurt was delayed and she missed her onward flight. Waiting for her and getting worried, I ended up going to the Lufthansa office in Bologna, which thankfully got hold of Julz, who was in the Lufthansa office in Frankfurt. I was keeping in touch with Julz's dad at the same time and was able to tell him what was going on. Eventually a very tired and stressed Julz arrived at Bologna, and we made our way to Bologna station for the ninety-minute journey to Rimini. This time I remembered to validate the tickets!

Julz arrived just in time for the first concert of the session. Annoyingly for her, and purely coincidentally, three of the arias featured were from *Don Carlo*. Having spent much of the year watching the rehearsals, Julz knew the opera well, so much so that while the arias were being sung in Italian, she was mouthing back the words in English.

One of the attractions of the course that year was that it now included master classes with three very important singers: Katia Ricciarelli, Wilma Vernocchi, and Luciano Pavarotti. For the Pavarotti master class, there were to be auditions to decide who would get to sing for him. In order to prepare for mine, I worked with a principal bass from Verona Arena, Alessandro Calamai.

Julz came with me to my lesson, and Alessandro asked her to sing a song she knew. Hearing her speak, he felt that she had a good singing voice. She blushed a little and sung a little of "Somewhere" from *West Side Story*. Julz still states that she cannot sing, but both I and Alessandro disagreed! The lessons went well, as did the audition for the Pavarotti master class: I was delighted to discover that I was one of those selected.

Julz's birthday came, and we had dinner together in the main square in Rimini, Piazza de Tre Martiri. It was her twenty-first birthday, and I bought her a necklace with a small diamond. We decided we would tease her family, as Tara, her elder sister, had been betting that we were going to get engaged. Julz told her I had given her a diamond and left her to wonder for a few days before putting her out of her misery. It was a wonderful evening, and I knew I would be sad when the time came for her to return to Wales.

With Julz by my side, I worked hard to prepare to sing in front of Pavarotti. The day of the master class came very quickly. I had practised a number of arias, but the one I really wanted to sing was "Che Gelida Manina" from *La Bohème*. It was my favourite, and the words, which I had first translated the previous year, made me melt:

> Two thieves: beautiful eyes, have stolen all my treasure.
> They entered with you just now, and now all my dreams
> are second hand. But the theft doesn't bother me, because
> here in this room with you I find hope.

Carlo, the *répétiteur*, told me that "Che Gelida Manina" was a risky choice as Rodolfo was the role Pavarotti had performed most, so he would know it like the back of his hand. I was insistent, however, that it was the aria I wanted to do. I knew it was a risk, but sing it I would.

The master class was originally to have taken place at the opera house in Longiano, where I had earlier done a concert. It was moved to the regular venue in San Leo, which I was a little disappointed about, as I thought the acoustics in the small opera house in Longiano were perfect. It was a thrill to see Pavarotti in person; he was a warm and kindly presence, and took his seat in the auditorium to hear us sing.

I watched the other singers perform as Pavarotti listened and gave out a few pieces of advice. By the time it was my turn, I was very nervous. Julz had been there the whole time, holding my hand while I waited to sing, and I could feel she was shaking every bit as much as I was. Here I was, about to perform in front of the most well-known tenor in the world. What would he think of my singing? Would he like it? I really hoped so. He had a surprisingly soft and gentle voice. He seemed relaxed and to enjoy being there.

Despite the situation, my singing started confidently enough and I found myself getting into the performance. Then I found myself coming to the most challenging part of the piece, where the high C arrives. Because of my nerves, I didn't take a breath where I normally did. Although I sang the high C fairly well, I only barely made it to the end of the phrase. I finished, and waited to hear what Pavarotti had to say. To my delight, he was smiling.

"Very good," he said, in English. "I liked it. Just one thing, though. Rodolfo wouldn't have run out of breath there. He would have been feeling breathless because he'd have wanted to put his arms around Mimi; he would certainly be breathless at the end."

Then he asked, "What else do you sing?"

"'Nessun Dorma,'" I replied. This made Pavarotti raise his eyebrows and smile some more. I listed some of the arias I sang. "'Io Lo Vido.' 'E Lucevan le Stelle . . .'"

"Ah," Pavarotti interrupted. "Sing me 'E Lucevan le Stelle.'"

I felt privileged, because I was the only person whom he had asked to sing twice. I sang "E Lucevan le Stelle" from *Tosca*, and once again Pavarotti was full of praise for my performance. I was delighted. At the end of the class a group photo was taken with Pavarotti, but being fairly short and not very pushy, I can't be seen in the picture at all. It didn't matter—my memories of what he said to me about my singing were enough. The evening had flown by, and after a great dinner in one of the small trattorias in the middle of nowhere, it was time, all too soon, to help Julz pack. She was going home the next day.

The rest of the course went past in something of a blur—we did a master class with Katia Ricciarelli, who was very complimentary about my voice. (Apparently Katia did not get on with Pavarotti, and we were told not to mention anything he'd said!) I also performed at another concert in San Leo, singing the finale of *Don Carlo* in Italian and a large part of the first act of *La Bohème*. Before I knew it, it was time to head home—and back to Julz.

The date I was flying home was 11 September 2001. Julz came to meet me at the airport. She'd taken the coach, as she didn't fancy driving into the London area, and had parked her car in Bridgend, at the shopping outlet. As we picked the car up and drove through the Maesteg valley, we listened to the radio in disbelief. The news had broken that a plane had hit the twin towers in New York. We sat in the car in stunned silence. Was it an accident? If not, why would anyone do such a thing? It didn't bear thinking about.

When we got back to Julz's parents in the village of Bryn on the outskirts of Port Talbot, the day's events were unfolding on the television screen. We watched footage of the planes striking the towers and then saw the shocking sight of the buildings collapsing. The people in those buildings had left home that morning expecting it to be a normal day, and now their loved ones would never see them again. It really brought home to us the fragility of life and how quickly things could change.

The events galvanized something within me. The next day, I asked Julz if she would like to start looking at rings. To my relief and joy, she didn't look too shocked and just said, "Okay."

We went into Swansea, and it didn't take long to find the perfect ring: we instinctively knew it was the right one the moment it went onto Julz's finger. It was an eighteen-carat gold with a twist and a quarter-carat diamond. As she placed it on her left ring finger, I saw the joy in Julz's eyes. I knew she didn't want to give the ring up. As far as she was concerned, it was already hers. Julz told me that taking the ring off was one of the most difficult things she'd ever had to do.

But I didn't have much money left after the trip to Italy, so I had to put a deposit on the ring instead of buying it outright. I would go to the store every month and pay a little more towards it. I couldn't help but think how lucky I was to have such a beautiful, funny, and intelligent girlfriend, who by Christmas would be my fiancée. I wanted to tell it to the world, but I needed to start saving up money first, not just for the ring but for the wedding itself.

I proposed to Julz on the seafront at Mumbles. It had only been ten months since we had met and come here on our first date, but this did not feel rushed. Our union felt like it had always been intended. Already, Julz was a great foil for me, and I was delighted when she said yes.

STRUGGLES

Julz and I decided to tell our families about the engagement at Christmas. Right from the start, I had got on well with Julz's family. On first meeting them, I remarked with surprise on meeting someone who was one of eighteen children. Her dad, Dave, turned and said, "What of it?" The penny dropped: Julz had already told me that her mum was one of seventeen, and I had forgotten this. That was the first of many laughs at my expense, and they still continue. I immediately felt confident that I would be welcomed as one of them. Her mum reminded me of my own mum, and I sensed that her dad and I would become friends. Her grancha reminded me of my own—the fact that he had been in the same pits as my grancha intrigued both Dave and me.

Christmas seemed to take forever to come. I wanted it to be here now, and I wanted it to be completely happy. Finally, it was Christmas Eve, and Julz and I had dinner together before we headed to the midnight service at All Saints in Fishponds, ready to tell our news.

I wanted my parents to love Julz as much as I did. While Mum was her ever-present mild-mannered self who would always try and get on with anyone, Dad wasn't so easy about our engagement, and always disagreed with us spending the weekend together. While I could tell Mum was happy (her attitude was that if I was happy, she was happy), I could also sense that my father was much less than pleased. However, his attitude did change once we got married. Julz's parents had already accepted me as one of their own. I wondered whether that would ever be fully true of my own parents. Julz was the most important thing in my life now, and nothing was going to change that.

We both did what we could to spend as much time together as possible. I was still on Bristol City Council, and Julz would truly show her love by sitting through a five-hour full council meeting. She worked at an insurance call centre and was giving up her day off to spend time with me. She was bored rigid, but this certainly convinced me of her love!

I had started working in Tesco's home shopping department, which basically meant I did other people's shopping for them. This had its advantages, despite its early start time at six in the morning: I finished work at one on Saturday afternoons, so I could be with Julz earlier in the day. Often there would be engineering works on the train line to Wales, and since rail replacement buses wouldn't accept bikes, it meant I would cycle the thirty-plus miles via the cycle track on the older of the two Severn bridges to get the train at Newport. On the way back, I would catch the 0349 train from Port Talbot to Bristol Parkway, and then cycle from the parkway to Tesco. It was exhausting, but worth it to see Julz.

I was singing a little less now, and concentrating more on saving up to get married and finding somewhere to live. But I hadn't stopped entirely, despite my father's fears. I took the roles of Don Basilio and Don Ottavio on Bath Opera's productions of Mozart's *Marriage of Figaro* and *Don Giovanni*. These were enjoyable performances in different parts of the area surrounding Bath and Wiltshire.

I also had an audition for English National Opera's Baylis Programme. Julz supported my going for the course, even though it meant delaying our honeymoon if I was selected. This was a workshop audition in front of a panel that included the renowned vocal expert Mary King. The singing went well, but these situations where I had to interact with others always made me anxious. In the end, I just missed out on a place; but I was first reserve, which was a good achievement in itself, as places on the course were highly sought after.

Although I didn't pass that audition, I was to have more success elsewhere. First, Bath Opera held auditions for its main production in 2003: Verdi's *Aida*. I went for the main tenor role, Radames, and to my joy, despite there being plenty of competition for the part, I got it. Even better, an audition came up for a production in North London for a Puccini opera, *Manon Lescaut*. I had decided that, within reason, I would travel anywhere to do a Puccini role. Julz drove me to Southgate for the audition, and after a few days I heard that I had got that part, too. I was thrilled. Suddenly, the first half of 2003 was looking extremely exciting—two operas and a wedding!

With all that going on, the next few months were going to be a busy time for me. And that was before everything that happened next.

CHAPTER TEN

An Opera and an Op

I STARTED FEELING UNWELL during rehearsals for *Aida* and *Manon Lescaut*. It began with a dull ache in my stomach, and at first I figured I had a bad stomach: something simple like food not agreeing with me. But when I went to London to do some Christmas shopping, I realized the pain could be something more serious.

This should have been a enjoyable occasion; the Christmas lights were on, and London's shopping streets were bustling with people excited about the festive season. But the pain in my stomach was getting worse, and I had to walk with a pronounced limp to cope. I knew then that something was terribly wrong.

When I got back from London, I immediately took time off from work. I got on my bike, cycled to Bristol Parkway, and caught the train to Julz's parents' house. All I knew was that if I was going to be ill, then I wanted to be with Julz. I wanted to be able to see her, and for her to not have to drive all the way to Bristol.

STRUGGLES

Like many men, I hated going to doctors. But by now the pain had become unbearable, and I was forced to go to Bryn surgery. The doctor there told me that as I'd had the pain for over a week, it was unlikely to be appendicitis. But to be on the safe side, he referred me to Princess of Wales Hospital in Bridgend.

At the hospital I was seen by the surgical registrar. As I explained my symptoms, he reiterated the local doctor's opinion that after a week, appendicitis was unlikely.

"If it was," he said cheerfully, "you'd be dead by now!"

I wasn't sure whether to be relieved or worried by that comment.

"I suppose I should rule it out completely, though," the registrar continued. "Have you noticed your breath smelling at all?"

This, apparently, is a well-known symptom of appendicitis.

I shook my head. "I brushed my teeth before heading out," I explained.

"Of course," the registrar replied. "But can you blow into my face anyway, to be sure?"

As I breathed out, the registrar winced.

"That breath could knock over a donkey! Yes, I'm afraid it probably is appendicitis. We're going to have to operate pretty quickly."

In modern hospitals, appendectomy is normally a keyhole surgical procedure. In my case, because I had left it so long, my appendix had actually burst. The surgeon, the registrar cheerfully told me, was going to have to "cut me up" to take it out. I was nervous at the thought, but they knew best.

I was relieved that I had made the decision to come to Wales, as I definitely wanted to be close to Julz if I was having an operation. The news didn't go down so well with my parents, who felt it was inconsiderate of me to have gone over, knowing they would have to travel. I didn't do it to put them out; Julz was my future wife, and I wanted to be close to her. I thought they would understand, but I don't think they did.

Thankfully, the operation went with no hitches and I was sewn up pretty tidily. I was still in pain, however, and had regular doses of pethidine (aka Demerol) to deal with it. As Christmas ticked closer, I worried that I would have to stay in over the festive period. But after five days in hospital, I was finally discharged and allowed to go home. I was glad to have put the whole episode behind me.

Or so I thought.

I'd got through Christmas fine, and thought I had been convalescing well. Then just before New Year, Julz and I went to watch a film at the cinema in the Aberavon seafront. Everything seemed normal: we had our usual snack of peanut M&M's and settled down to watch the movie. But as the film went on, I started to feel less and less with it. I was beginning to feel sick and dizzy.

Vomiting is something I've always hated, but by the time we got back to Julz's parents' place, I couldn't stop myself. I was violently sick several times. Julz drove me to Maesteg Hospital to see the off-hours doctors, who immediately referred me back to the Princess of Wales Hospital in Bridgend. By now I was being sick so violently that it hurt.

It was déjà vu: I was readmitted to the ward I had left little over a week ago and saw the same doctor as before. I was sent for tests and a CT scan to check for infection. There were a few ominous mutterings and I was sent to another room, where I was given an ultrasound scan. By now I was getting more than a little worried. The gel felt a bit weird on my skin, but more disconcerting were the words from the person operating the scanner. I couldn't pick up many of them, but two in particular leapt out: tumour and malignant.

I was left panicking. It was hours before I next saw a doctor, the same surgical registrar I had seen on my first admission. This time around, he was somewhat more serious as he gave me the results.

"We've found a tumour, Paul," he said. "It's close to your liver, and it's large. We think it's about thirty centimetres in length."

"Is it malignant?" I asked, remembering what I'd seen on the scanner.

"We won't know for certain until it has been removed. But we suspect it's benign."

The registrar told me they couldn't do the operation there, and I would have to have surgery in the University Hospital of Wales in Cardiff. At this point, Mum and Dad, who'd rushed over to see me, came in. I got an earful from my father, who told me I should be seen in Bristol, not here in the backwater that was Wales.

"I can refer you to Bristol if you want," the registrar offered. "Though it will be quicker to be referred through Bridgend, as you're already on the emergency list. If you transfer to Bristol, you'll have to be assessed all over again."

"I have no intention of transferring," I told my father.

He was still angry, so I told him that if he couldn't calm down, then he should leave. This was the first time in a long time that I had stood up for myself, and although I felt ill, it made me feel a little stronger as a person.

I was discharged on New Year's Day. I returned for regular

appointments with the hospital's consultants, who told me it would be better if I was operated on as soon as possible. A date was found for the middle of March, right in between the performances of *Aida* and *Manon Lescaut*. I asked whether it was all right to carry on singing and take part in the shows and was told that although I wasn't fit to work, I was fine to take part in the productions, provided I didn't exert myself too much.

The performances of *Aida* took place at the end of February and the beginning of March. With everything else going on, the shows seemed to come around quickly. My role as Radames was a very challenging one, but I was determined to sing it. The rest of the cast was no gentler with me in spite of what was ahead; during the opera, I was thrown on the floor and against a throne so hard that the back of my legs were marked.

A week later, I had a meeting with the surgeon. He told me that as the tumour was on the right-hand side of my body, there was a very real risk of cutting through a major artery. As a result, they would have to stop my breathing and put me on a ventilator. On top of this, the surgeon explained that they would need to thread the breathing line through my vocal cords.

My initial thought was, You're going to do *what?* Followed by, What if they can't start me up again? and, Why me? The surgeon noticed my look of horror and told me not to worry: they knew I was a singer and would take every care not to do any damage. He added, though, that their first priority was to make sure I stayed alive. I came away in no doubt of how serious this operation was, and the risks involved.

It was a lot to take in. I was still trying to do so as I made my way to London for that night's *Manon Lescaut* rehearsal. I spoke to Southgate Opera's musical director, Neil Cloake, about it. To my horror, he told me his wife had had the same procedure and it had left her unable to sing for a considerable time. This, of course, did nothing to settle my nerves.

The operation was now upon me. I went up to the hospital the day before and settled into the pre-operation ward, where I spent some time with Julz and her parents before they left for home. The following day, Julz returned to see me in the morning, as the operation wasn't until around noon. I was given an ECG to ensure that everything was working as it should, and then I was given my pre-meds.

I had heard of pre-meds before, but didn't know exactly what they were. I started to feel very drowsy. As they were wheeling me towards the theatre, I felt someone fiddling with my back, and a man introduced himself. He told me that he was normally an ambulance technician, but was on job swap for the day. He wanted to know if he had put my epidural in the right place. By now I wasn't really on the same planet.

"You'll know better than m . . ." I said, before going under.

The next thing I remember is coming around to find tubes coming out of me left, right, and centre. I was now in the high-dependency unit of the hospital, and everything was being monitored. Every few minutes I felt a fibre band go tight on my arm; so tightly it almost hurt.

The first thing I did was call for Julz. I didn't want anything else at that time: just Julz. I was told that she had called to check on me and was told I was "comfortable," a medical euphemism if ever there was one. I wasn't so sure about the "comfortable" prognosis, especially when the strong painkillers stopped working. I had a large post-op scar that felt like it was on fire. As time went on, the sensation changed, and not for the better. It now felt like I had a full express train on my chest. I had never known pain like it.

I wanted to scream, but I didn't want to be a wimp. I didn't press the buzzer for assistance, but in the end the monitor readings did that for me. A nurse came in and asked if I was okay.

"I'm fine," I lied.

"Strange," the nurse said, looking at the equipment, "your blood pressure and heart rate are telling a different story."

I shuffled in the bed a little. I wasn't actually all that good at playing the hard man, but I was determined to do my best. The nurse, though, was determined to get an answer.

"On a scale of one to ten, how is the pain?"

I gave my answer considerable thought.

"Ooh . . . about thirty."

The nurse got me to lean forward so she could check my epidural. She frowned at me.

"Why didn't you press the call button?"

I shrugged my shoulders. "I didn't want to be any trouble."

The nurse sighed. "The reason you're in pain is that the epidural hasn't been put in properly. You are lying there with precisely zero pain relief. Let me get the pain nurse, and we'll see if we can't get you feeling more comfortable."

I had visions of a nurse dressed in black leathers and leather gloves, but she wasn't that kind of pain nurse. The decision was made to put me on self-administered morphine, and I was given strict instructions to make sure I gave myself enough of the drug, and not simply suffer in silence. I had been warned that I might get strange dreams, but this didn't happen—perhaps I didn't take enough! I asked if Julz could visit and was told this shouldn't be a problem since I was now alert and awake.

I ended up staying in the high-dependency unit for a few days, then transferred to a surgical ward while I recovered. I was "nil by mouth" for over a week: I wasn't allowed any food or drink, all my body's essential needs provided for by the drip in my arm. As Murphy's Law would have it, while I was not allowed to eat, every single lunch and dinner on the ward smelled delicious. Steak and mushroom pie, lasagne . . . my mouth was watering, but I wasn't allowed any of it.

At the time of my operation, the Second Gulf War had just started. Being unable to sleep most of the time, I sat there and watched the events as they unfolded. Even when I did get to sleep, it was not undisturbed. The medication I was on, and the fact that I was not eating anything at all, upset my system. I felt very low and was in considerable pain. The latter wasn't helped by the decision to remove the morphine. The nurses had been keeping me under review and had noticed that I didn't take many breaths per minute. One of the undesirable side effects of morphine, they told me, was not breathing often enough and therefore suffering from oxygen deprivation. In fact, I was breathing quite normally for me. As a singer I was used to taking long, deep, slow breaths, and I tried to explain this to them. Their minds were made up, however, and I was moved on to oral painkillers.

Coming off the morphine just made the pain worse. I repeatedly woke up in the night from the agony. The first night it happened, I asked for pain relief, thinking the night nursing staff would get me painkillers that wouldn't affect my main dose. I thought wrong: the nurse brought forward *half* my next dose, but wrote it up as a full dose. This meant that for the first eight hours of the next day I had no pain relief at all.

It wasn't until the end of my second week on the ward that the pain settled down a little, and I started to get into a more normal routine. The tramadol was starting to be a little more effective, although I still had a fair amount of pain to deal with. I also had to cope with the fact that my wound was open, weeping, and infected. Although I was no longer nil by mouth, the menu had changed and the mouth-watering food I dreamt of had been taken off. Instead of steak pie I was served liver and onions, something I'd had more than enough of as a child.

Eighteen days after entering the hospital, I was discharged into the care of a district nurse. She would help me with medication and with changing dressings. But when I left, I still didn't know whether the tumour was cancerous or not. The relief of good news would not come until several weeks later.

I was determined not to let my illness get in the way of my singing. The day after I was discharged, auditions were being held for the chorus of the Welsh National Opera. If I was honest with myself, I wasn't at all ready. Ian Comboy, my voice teacher, also told me exactly the same thing. As with his comments about taking part in the singing competition in Barcelona, his advice was absolutely right. As with Barcelona, I ignored it. Too late, I thought to myself. I'm outside their rehearsal doors now.

On reflection, it was a mixture of stupidity combined with a good pinch of stubbornness that led me to go ahead with the audition. It was a stupid thing to do because it could mark my card for the future, and prevent me getting anywhere in subsequent auditions. I also didn't help myself with my selection of music: I had chosen "Che Gelida Manina" and "E Lucevan le Stelle," even though the letter of invitation indicated that I should pick from different genres. However, most of my music was in Bristol, so this was the only choice I had.

In the rehearsal with the pianist beforehand, I was in very good form and quite confident. But it all fell apart in the audition room. I had used all my energy in preparing and didn't sing well. I made my apologies, explaining that I had only been discharged from hospital the previous day. The panel told me that although they could hear some potential, I should have waited until I was well again before auditioning.

My focus now was getting ready for the production of *Manon Lescaut*; it was only a week before a full weekend of staged rehearsals at Southgate, North London, and I needed to learn my words. I used my Sony microphone to record my voice over the top of José Carreras's and listened to it on repeat. I then got some reference cards and wrote down the libretto again and again until I could write it out without looking at the music score. This was my system for learning lyrics, and remains so to this day.

During the whole time I was rehearsing with Southgate Opera, members of the chorus were kind enough to put me up in their homes, instead of my having to travel back and forth from Wales. One particular family that looked after me very well was the Prior family. They had three cute little girls who would fight over whose Choco Shreddies I would be given.

When they heard my surname, they were immediately reminded of *Chitty Chitty Bang Bang* and Caractacus Potts. I was serenaded by all three to a pitch-perfect performance of "Truly Scrumptious." The youngest, a very precocious four-year-old, was a huge fan of James Bond music and sang a very sweet version of "Nobody Does It Better." The people of Southgate Opera treated me very well, and I had a brief but enjoyable time with them.

The rehearsals were quite intensive and not helped by the fact I was still recovering from my operation. I was partway through rehearsing the first love scene with Ruth Kerr, who was playing the title role, when she noticed that something wasn't quite right.

"Oh my God, Paul, you're bleeding!"

I told everyone not to worry and explained that I had an open wound and simply needed to change my dressing. They weren't convinced when I returned, but I was insistent. There was no way I was giving up. I was determined to perform my role in full.

And get through it I just about did. One of each cast's performances was filmed, and in the footage of the finale of act 4, I could be seen limping slightly. This could be considered good acting, as I was meant to be in the desert, dying of thirst. I had succeeded through stubbornness and sheer determination—I was proud of myself.

There were certain sections of my performance that Julz couldn't watch. At one point, the action called for me to kiss Manon. I assured Julz that it was just acting, but she wasn't so sure.

"You don't need to look like you're enjoying it that much, though!" she said with a half smile.

Ian Comboy had suggested I write to music agents and invite them to all the performances. I did, but never heard back from any of them. Despite that, my performance in the role of Chevalier des Grieux was one of the highlights of my life.

I had one final leading role to perform that spring—the bridegroom at my wedding to Julz. Our marriage was to be the culmination of a frantic few months: as well as my time in hospital and the opera productions, we had also been house hunting and had finally found our first home. The house was in central Port Talbot, and though it wasn't in great condition, it was the best we could afford. When we applied for the mortgage, we could only use Julz's income: we didn't know whether my tumour was cancerous or not, and as a result I couldn't get critical illness coverage or life insurance. We had a very nervous wait while our house, which was a repossession, went through its statutory ten-day notice period. After an agonizing wait, we discovered that our offer was the only one accepted within the notice period. We were delighted: it was the last property in the area we could have bought with our budget. Now we could focus on getting married.

The morning that greeted our wedding day, 24 May 2003, was a gloomy one. It threatened rain, but somehow that didn't seem to matter. Along with my best man, Mark Shovelton, with whom I'd worked for years at Tesco, I headed to the church: St. Cynwyd's Church in Llangynwyd, or as it's known in the area, Llan. Next to the church is a monument recognizing one of the most romantic stories in the area. A landowner's daughter was courting a local lad against the will of her father. When her father locked her away, she used leaves and her own blood to write to her lover. Opposite the church, one of the oldest in Wales, stands the oldest pub in the country, suitably called The Old House. It was one of our favourite pubs for food, and a fitting place for my last pint as a "free man."

It was time to head over to the church and wait for my beautiful bride. And how beautiful she looked that day, her skin glistening and her long wavy hair resting on her shoulders, as I looked into her eyes. I couldn't believe my good fortune. Here I was, about to marry the girl of my dreams. It was more than I had expected or, to my mind, deserved.

When the time came to say our vows, I felt like I was waiting to go on stage. I had to fight every part of me that wanted to burst into tears. It was all I could do not to break down into a gibbering wreck. Julz, as ever, seemed so much more composed than I was. She had glided gracefully down the aisle, whereas I was concerned I would trip and land on my face. She said her vows, too, with an effortlessness that made me wonder at her composure.

With the vows over came the signing of the registers. This made it official—we were now man and wife! Julz's colleagues at Admiral Insurance had suggested we combine her name and mine to make a double-barrelled surname, but we knew they were joking, really. After all, Mrs. Cooper-Potts would look far too much like Copper-Potts!

While we were signing the registers, Judy Davis, who had played *Aida* in the Bath Opera production, got up to sing "Ave Maria," accompanied on the organ by Peter Blackwood, Bath Opera's musical director. After I finished signing the registers, Peter accompanied me as I sang a song to Julz. While playing the parts of Radames and des Grieux were challenging and nerve-wracking, this was the most important performance of my life, and I felt it.

The song was Edward Grieg's "Ich Liebe Dich"—"I Love Thee." It was all I could do to hold myself together, and there were many moments when I struggled to stop myself from crying. I could see my beautiful bride doing what brides do, blushing and wiping away a few tears. I meant every word I sang. It was a special moment on a special day.

Then it was time for us to leave the church. We had entered as Mr. Potts and Miss Cooper, and were leaving as Mr. and Mrs. Potts. I still had to pinch myself; there had been so many times when I doubted this day would ever come. As the confetti rained down to seal this memorable day, I felt like the luckiest man in the world.

CHAPTER ELEVEN

In Sickness and in Health

"*S*ANT'AGNELLO, *per favore.*"

It was six days after our wedding, and Julz and I had arrived at Naples International Airport to begin our honeymoon. We'd booked a fortnight on the Neapolitan Riviera, which we'd spent more than a year saving up for, and for which Julz's mum and dad had kindly contributed what they could afford. As the taxi driver loaded our luggage in the boot (trunk), we climbed into the car, eager to get there and unpack. As the taxi left the airport for the Riviera, and I chatted to the driver in Italian. I explained how we'd managed to get a great deal on a five-star hotel on the edge of Sorrento, in a village called Sant'Agnello. It was such a good deal that even the travel agent was surprised, and had to double-check the price. The driver was really friendly and gave us lots of tips that would save us money.

"The only worthwhile trip with the travel rep is the Amalfi Drive," he advised us. "And make sure you sit on the right-hand side of the coach so you have a view of the water."

He told us, too, that the guides at Pompeii were often unkind to people if they couldn't keep up with the rest of the group. We later witnessed exactly that, with an elderly lady being reduced to tears, having paid handsomely for the privilege.

Julz and I visited both Pompeii and Herculaneum, and found them fascinating. The only trip we organized through the travel rep was the Amalfi Drive, but the tour wasn't booked properly, and so the pickup didn't happen. In the end, we took the service bus down to Amalfi, sitting on the right-hand side as recommended, and came back by boat, for less money than the rep's trip. There were sheer drops everywhere, but the views from the bus and the boat on the way back were incredible.

As it was our honeymoon, I didn't want to be too budget conscious, but we had to be aware of expenses. My knowledge of Italian was to save us money on more than one occasion. We went on a couple of mini-cruises round the Bay of Naples, one of them to the island of Capri. Capri was notoriously expensive, and when we arrived, there was a long queue for the funicular to the main part of the island. To get around this, there were taxi drivers with convertible cars. Knowing the Italian way, I chatted with one of the drivers in Italian, exchanging pleasantries and explaining that we were on honeymoon. When I asked the cost to the main square, we got a much cheaper price than did those asking in English.

As we drove along, Julz turned to me and said, "There you go, you got your ride in a car with the top down!"

I laughed, remembering how I had been disappointed with having the roof up on our wedding day because of the gloomy weather.

We also went on a mini-cruise to the island of Ischia. The boat stopped a few times to allow people to go swimming. I was aware that I needed to make sure I used plenty of sunblock on my wound, as it was getting a little red. We stopped in a bay, and I noticed a young boy throwing bread out into the sea, attracting jellyfish. Later on he started dive-bombing into the sea, jumping in with his knees tucked into his chest, getting people in the restaurant area soaked. He thought this was great fun. After one particularly heavy splash, he noticed the scar from my operation.

"Hey!" he shouted to get my attention. "How did that happen?"

"This?" I said trying to stop myself from laughing as an evil thought crossed my mind. "Oh, this was from when I was here last year, when I was bitten by a shark!"

He looked horrified, and refused to go back into the water. At least the people in the restaurant stayed dry after that.

We were well looked after at our hotel, having our meals in the restaurant every night as we were booked half-board. Our regular waiters were funny and friendly. I noticed that one in particular would flirt with the older ladies, and I teased him by calling him Don Giovanni, which is Italian for Don Juan or Casanova. On many evenings, Julz and I would go down to a local bar and have a few drinks with the waiters. We got on well with them, and they were impressed with my knowledge of their language.

Towards the end of the honeymoon, we were given a special meal by the hotel. The area is renowned for both its seafood and its tomatoes and buffalo mozzarella. Neither of these options worked for Julz, as she didn't fancy the seafood and hates tomatoes. This was before we went to Asia, where she learned to like seafood. It was a fantastic meal, which ended with Crêpes Suzette prepared at the table by "Don Giovanni."

Julz and I really enjoyed our two weeks in the sun, but before too long it was time to head home. Time to return to reality—and I wasn't looking forward to it. I was due to start back at Tesco within a week. It was going to be a routine of 3 a.m. wake-up calls, except rather than being just once a week, they would now be a daily occurrence.

I was exhausted just thinking about it, but there was no way round it. I was nearly out of company sick pay entitlement, and we now had a mortgage to pay. At the wedding, I had been warned by some of Julz's extended family that I would need to look after her now, and that I should consider whether we could afford for me to continue activities that didn't earn money. We both knew what they were talking about. As we returned to Britain, I was very aware of my new responsibilities.

I always knew that going back to work would be a challenge, but I wasn't sure just how much of a challenge it would be. Getting up every day at 3:15 a.m. wasn't going to be easy, and initially it was a huge shock to my system, so much so that I was sick on my second day back.

I was offered the opportunity to return part-time, but this didn't make sense financially. Because I still had to pay my weekly season ticket on the train however many days I worked, it wouldn't have left me with enough money. I couldn't get a transfer while still off sick, so I knew I would have to live with this for a while. My situation, though, was going to get worse before it got better.

Four days after restarting work, I was cycling from Eastville to Bristol Parkway station to catch the train back to Wales. It was a warm, sunny July afternoon and I was looking forward to getting home. I was on Filton Avenue, about two-thirds of my way to the station, when a driver pulled out of a petrol station without looking. I had no time to stop or take evasive action, so all I could do was to squeeze as hard as I could on the brakes. It still wasn't enough—I went over the handlebars and put my hands out in front of me to try to break my fall.

I heard a crack, then I started feeling dizzy. I was aware that I was in shock. My shoulder appeared to be in a very strange position, but I couldn't feel a thing, so I pushed the bone back. I was dazed and wondering what was going on, and the driver came across and offered to take me to the local doctor. I told him he needed to call for the police and an ambulance. He ignored me and offered to take me to nearby Frenchay Hospital. Again, I insisted that his legal obligation was to report the accident to the police and to call an ambulance. He asked me if I was sure.

"I'm in shock," I told him, "but I'm not stupid! Please do what you're obliged to do."

As I waited for the ambulance, I started to feel my shoulder come painfully to life. I called Julz, who was alarmed and said her dad would come over to Bristol to pick me up. I was put into the ambulance and the medics tried to give me something for the pain. I tend to be a pincushion for needles, and they were unable to find a vein. They ended up offering me gas and air, otherwise known as nitrous oxide, or laughing gas. I hated it: the gas made me feel light-headed, sick, and out of control. I ended up removing the mask, preferring to suffer the pain even though it was by now close to unbearable.

At Frenchay, the doctors confirmed that I'd suffered a complicated fracture to my collarbone as well as severe whiplash. The collarbone is known to be one of the most painful bones to break, and I can certainly confirm the truth of this! For the first month after the accident, I barely slept at all. Whatever position was right for my shoulder was wrong for my neck, and vice versa.

This lack of sleep created complications with my post-operative state. Because of my previous operations, I now had only one adrenal gland; one of the jobs this gland does is to push cortisol around your body to help it deal with stress. After my operations earlier in the year, I had been put on hormone replacement therapy, to try to compensate until my remaining adrenal gland took up the workload of the one removed.

That hadn't happened yet, and because of the stress and lack of sleep, my body decided to completely give up. I stayed on the sofa downstairs for a month, all but not moving; I had no will or strength left to do anything. When I went to see my specialist at the hospital in Cardiff he increased my therapy, raising my prednisolone dose from 5 mg to 15 mg a day. I needed Julz's help to do anything, and this left me feeling powerless. Julz never complained, but I'm sure she felt she had done the "in sickness" part of the vows in advance, and was hoping the "health" part would soon come.

Money now became an issue. Once my sick pay ended, Julz and I would be living off just one wage. I didn't know how long I would be off sick, as the collarbone seemed determined not to heal. There was a very real chance I would need an operation to insert metal rods that would force my collarbone to heal. Before long, I found myself applying for incapacity benefit. We became more and more dependent on credit cards, just to keep going.

After the illness, the wedding, and the honeymoon, there were no savings left. We used credit cards to buy food, pay bills, pay our council tax and, in the end, we used them to pay our credit card bills. We used some equity in the house to try to pay off the cards, but it wasn't long before we ended up back at square one.

All the while, the warning of one of Julz's uncles was ringing in my ears: "You have to look after her now." Singing at this point was the very last thing on my mind. Julz didn't have the money to go out with her workmates. It was a struggle to even pay for the fuel she needed to drive to work. She had always been prepared to give up anything for me; I knew that now it was my turn to give up something in return. I couldn't put our house at risk in order to continue singing. I couldn't justify spending money on lessons and travel costs to and from Bath any longer. Already, other tenors were taking my place because I was unable to perform, but what could I do? I would have to wait until I returned to work to see if I could get back into it.

It was seven long, painful months before I could even contemplate going back to work. By then, Tesco was applying pressure, saying that I would have to consider going back part-time or else they would lay me off. I had been with them for ten years by this point, but this now meant nothing. I had been active in the Union of Shop, Distributive and Allied Workers (USDAW), but I felt that the area organiser seemed to be more on Tesco's side than mine. The company wanted me to return to work fifteen hours a week; I explained that once I had paid my weekly season ticket, I would effectively *be paying* to work. On top of which, if I went back part-time, I would lose my benefits because Julz was earning. I would only be eligible for incapacity benefit if I wasn't working at all. Once I was working part-time, we wouldn't qualify for any means-tested benefits, and there was no state help for travel to and from work.

In the end I went back full-time, even though I didn't feel ready. Either I would return full-time, or not at all. Part-time wasn't going to be realistic financially. I put in a transfer request for something closer to home as soon as I returned, but the only thing available was a part-time job in Swansea, working nights twenty hours a week. I felt I had no choice but to take this, even though I would be reliant on overtime to make my money up.

It was an eighteen-mile round trip, but I cycled to and from Swansea four times a week, leaving home at nine at night and climbing back into bed with Julz at four in the morning. If nothing else, it was getting me fit again. The trouble was that I couldn't get guaranteed overtime. The most lucrative night for me was Saturday evening, which, because I was still on old conditions (which were different from newer contracts), meant I would be paid double time plus night premium. The store, however, could have two people on newer contracts for the same price as me.

Without the overtime, there wasn't enough money coming in for us to survive, and our debts continued to grow. I had to find another position, so I decided to apply for a job at the department store Debenhams. Debenhams didn't pay as well as Tesco because my long service there meant I was high up the pay grades. Debenhams could only offer me part-time work, another twenty hours a week, but I decided to take the job anyway.

For a month and a bit, I was working nights at Tesco and days in Debenhams. It was tough. Some days I was cycling to Swansea at nine at night, cycling back at three in the morning, grabbing six hours sleep, and then cycling back to Swansea at ten—then cycling back home at four in the afternoon, only to leave again a few hours later. Debenhams was concerned about this and told me they couldn't allow me to do it permanently. I knew myself that it was unsustainable. I had to start looking for other employment.

Before applying for the Debenhams job, I had applied for a full-time job at the mobile phone retailer Carphone Warehouse. I had heard nothing in more than a month, so I assumed I was unsuccessful. Then, to my surprise, I got a call inviting me in for an interview. I phoned back explaining my situation and arranged the interview so I wouldn't need to say anything to Debenhams at this stage.

I went to Llanelli for my interview, and it went well. I was nervous about sales work as it was target based, with payment partly by sales commission, and I didn't want to be involved in pressure selling. I had been into another phone shop to enquire about jobs and it had felt a little like double-glazing selling, and that wasn't what I wanted to do. Even so, I was delighted to be offered a job, and was invited up to London for make-or-break training. This next stage of the process involved candidates staying in London for a two-week course. At the end of this, everyone took a test: those who got marks under 85 percent failed and their employment was terminated.

During the course, we each had to demonstrate a skill that others didn't know we had. I took a risk and sang the most well-known part of "Nessun Dorma" a capella. I felt nervous, but the alternative was to be made to dance, and this was the lesser of two evils. The whole centre seemed to go quiet when I sang. A few of the other people on our course used their Bluetooth phones to record my performance, and every time I entered the room they would play it back to me. It was amusing and I felt a little honoured, too, as it was done out of respect as well as out of a sense of fun.

I passed the course and left Tesco and Debenhams for my new job. I started work in a Carphone Warehouse branch round the corner from where I lived. It was a fairly large store, housed within a shopping mall owned by the local council. My co-workers were Paul and Toni; I got on particularly well with Paul, who lived with his wife round the corner from Julz's mum and dad.

I quickly gained a reputation for being able to persuade people to buy phones and packages without resorting to the hard sell. If customers didn't need what they were asking for, I would let them know. On one occasion I even talked a customer out of a package he had specifically asked for. By selling him what he needed rather than what he had asked for, I didn't win a £7,000 Tag Heuer watch. I was, however, one of the top sellers overall in the South Wales area between Newport and Haverfordwest, and was rewarded with an incentive trip to Kenya, to go on safari in the Masai Mara National Reserve with other employees.

It was a wonderful five-day trip, with early morning game

drives watching the sun rising over Mount Kilimanjaro. I found it absolutely breathtaking to watch all the wildlife, and I would call Julz on my mobile, drinking sundowners and watching the sunset. The trip was only marred by the fact that it coincided with the 7/7 bombings back in London. That affected us all, but especially those who worked in the capital and were worried about colleagues and friends.

My reputation as a seller helped me get into the company's management programme. I went on a few daylong courses in Cheltenham, where I did a reprise of the "unexpected talent" I had done on my induction course, and was eventually given a store to run for a few weeks. My first bite at management was at the branch in the centre of Bridgend. The company's area management was pleased with my progress there, and a month or two later I was promoted to store manager at one of the company's failing stores, on The Hayes in Cardiff.

The Hayes Cardiff branch had a reputation for being a quiet store. Indeed, when I arrived on my first day to do the handover audit, the manager I was taking over from was playing sudoku with one of the sales consultants! That branch turned out to be one of the lowest-performing stores in the whole company. My area manager asked me if I would be able to make a difference, and I told him that I would do my best. He knew me well enough to know I was serious about that statement.

After a brief period of observation, I saw what the problem was: attitude. Everybody who worked there, be they regular team members at the branch or those sent over from one of the busier branches, dismissed the branch as too quiet; they were convinced they would never make any money. The way I saw it was that if someone came into work with the attitude that they were going to fail, then of course they wouldn't sell very much.

I was convinced that if people started to see the glass as being half full rather than half empty, then they would start to make sales. I told staff that the store being less busy meant they had time to give people good, honest service. This meant that sales would stick, and there would be a great amount of repeat business.

I sent back anyone who came over with a defeatist attitude, and with new personnel, my ideas were able to break through. I encouraged my staff to get out from behind the counter, although I never went as far as giving away any of my own sales. I made it clear that they had to compete with me, too. The result was healthy competition amongst the staff. When I joined the store it was number 558 out of 570 stores. Within three months it was ranked second in the company; after that we consistently got top-ten positions in the company. Our position was based on what sales we were getting, measured against our targets.

But although I was good at motivating and leading by example, I remained hopeless at organization. I would always lose marks on store visits because things weren't as organized as they should be.

Travelling to Cardiff and back was still a struggle, both in terms of time and also financially. Because the results were good, my area manager was prepared to subsidise my travel costs in order for me to stay at the branch. But when a branch manager's job became available at my original branch in Port Talbot, I had a decision to make. It was a difficult one, but I wanted to spend time at home with Julz.

I moved to the Port Talbot branch in November 2006. Again, I was soon making steady progress in the store, and trying to change attitudes there. Despite the commuting having come down, I was still working long hours and not enjoying any kind of social life. I was also constantly mourning the loss of my singing. I wondered whether I would ever sing in public again. I was barely able to sing at home, as we had next-door neighbours with young children and thin walls, and I was rarely home early enough to sing without disturbing them. At this point, I saw no future in singing at all.

Late one night, while doing emails and working on figures on the computer, I came across a pop-up window. I tried to close it down, but ended up maximizing it instead. In front of me I saw Simon Cowell inviting people to apply to take part in a new ITV show called *Britain's Got Talent*. I briefly looked at the video clip and read on.

Despite myself, I started filling in the online form. I didn't know where it would lead, and as I typed in the details I wondered why I was bothering. I stared at my reflection in the laptop screen. What the hell was I doing? Almost out loud, I asked myself why they would ever pick me. I sang the wrong kind of music; I was too ugly, too fat, and too old. To me, I was everything they were *not* looking for. I got to the end of the application and reached the option to send or cancel. I truly didn't know what to do. I didn't want to be one of those contestants people laughed at.

Yet another quiet voice inside me was telling me that I would never know unless I tried. I noticed that the entries closed the following morning, so just leaving it and coming back later was not an option. I decided to leave it up to chance. Picking up a ten-pence piece, I decided to play heads or tails: if it landed on heads I would submit the application; if it landed on tails I would close the pop-up window and never think about it again.

I threw the coin in the air and it landed . . .

. . . *Heads!*

The journey could now begin. I was still convinced that it would lead nowhere. But I hit send, and would have to wait and see.

To my surprise, I got a letter inviting me to audition. Julz got a surprise, too, as it was she who opened it, and I hadn't even told her I had applied. I hadn't mentioned it because I expected to fail.

I could still fail—the audition was on a Saturday, the seventeenth of March. In retail, Saturdays are the busiest day, and there was no way I could just take the day off. Richard, my colleague, was on holiday that week and offered to come in, but I didn't want him getting in trouble with his wife for something that would most likely amount to nothing.

In the end, my part-timer Alison Thorne heard what was happening. She told me she could get a child-minder and would be willing to come in for me. Alison was a lifesaver. There was no way *Britain's Got Talent* was going change the audition date to a Sunday, so her intervention saved the day. I had my chance. The question was, would I be able to make something of it?

PART THREE

Success

CHAPTER TWELVE

Britain's Got Talent

A s I DESCRIBED in the prologue, the amazing response I received for my *Britain's Got Talent* audition was difficult to take in. I stood there on the stage, feeling bemused at the reaction I'd just received. Especially from the judges: had Piers Morgan just said I had an "incredible voice"? Had Simon Cowell really just described my singing as "absolutely fantastic"?

I didn't have much time to think about their comments. As soon as I came offstage, the crew guide took me over to the show's hosts, Anthony "Ant" McPartlin and Declan "Dec" Donnelly, to record an interview. Ant and Dec, as the duo are known, are two of the biggest TV personalities in the UK, and this was the first time I had met them.

"So come on, Paul," they asked, "how do you feel?"

To be honest, I was so stunned that I didn't know how I felt. I hadn't been expecting anything at all from the audition, and had only felt confident about one thing: that I wasn't what they were looking for. I certainly hadn't anticipated the response my singing got. I was elated, but extremely confused.

Everyone I spoke to from ITV, by contrast, talked as though my success was a given. I did another interview in which the cameraman asked me repeatedly whether I thought I would win the whole competition.

"After that performance, and that reaction, surely you think you have a good chance?"

"I don't know," I replied resolutely. "I'll just take each step as it comes."

The one thing I didn't want to do was get ahead of myself. I had no idea what the next step would be after the audition; this was the first time the show had been on TV, and I wasn't sure how the competition would unfold. I didn't want to raise my hopes, for fear they might be dashed at the next stage.

I finished the interviews and went to find Julz and my family. They were ecstatic.

"See?" Julz hugged me. "I told you that you could do it!"

Julz, my family, and I headed out to Cardiff Bay to find a restaurant, and I allowed myself a bit of a celebration. It had been a good day—better than I could ever have expected. My thoughts, though, were already turning to the future, and I wondered what was going to happen next.

I returned to work on the Monday morning and thanked Alison for covering for me. I told everyone about the audition, and they wanted to know what the next stage was.

It was a strange couple of weeks, going from the highs of the audition to returning to the day job. It seemed ironic, too, that here I was, waiting for a phone call, all the while working in a shop selling phones! I had to concentrate, keep my feet on the ground, and get on with my work. We had targets at the store, and we still weren't quite hitting them.

After a fortnight or so, I finally got the call from the TV show's production team. I needed to go up to London for the next stage of the competition. The remaining contestants were put up in local hotels and had to report to the Grand Connaught Rooms in central London first thing on a Sunday morning. The production team warned me that it was likely to be a long day. I should make sure that I made myself comfortable and also bring refreshments, as they didn't know what would be provided.

The Grand Connaught Rooms were a venue that lived up to its name: several hundred years old, their opulent halls have played host to the likes of Elle Style Awards and Ralph Lauren shows. This particular Sunday, the rooms were full of two hundred nervous contestants and three judges who would decide our fate. The day began with a briefing from Simon Cowell, Piers Morgan, and Amanda Holden. We were told they had to get the numbers down from two hundred to just twenty-four for the live shows. They were going to go into another room and make the difficult decision as to who would get to compete. All we could do was wait.

It was a long day. With so many acts sitting there waiting, it soon got quite warm in the hall. There were accusations later from some of the eliminated acts that they had been denied permission to leave. I didn't find that to be true. When I asked the production team if I could get something to eat, they had no problem with my going out. As far as I could see, they just wanted to make sure they knew where everyone was.

The day wore on as we waited for the judges to reach their decision. Various bits of filming took place: Ant and Dec, complete with camera crew, went round the room chatting to the contestants; so, too, did Stephen Mulhern, the presenter of the accompanying ITV2 show *Britain's Got More Talent*. Then, finally, the wait was over: the judges had made up their minds. We were called for in groups of ten to go and discover our fate.

It was towards the end of the night when my name was called, along with nine others. We were taken by one of the researchers to the nearby Shaftesbury Theatre, where Piers, Amanda, and Simon were waiting for us. On the way to the theatre, we passed some of the other contestants, who had already seen the judges and been told they were unsuccessful. That didn't do much for the nerves, I can tell you!

The researcher took us into the theatre through the stage door and led us up onto the stage. In front of us were the judges: this was to be the moment of truth, and we were all dreading it. As well as myself, there was the young baton twirler Craig Womersley, one of the nicest people you could ever meet; and Bessie Cursons, the precocious musical theatre singer.

The fact that we weren't going to be performing again made the situation feel even more difficult. There was nothing we could now do to influence the judges' decision. To make matters worse, they decided to play a game of suspense with us.

Amanda spoke first. "We were all very impressed by your performances, but I'm afraid to tell you that . . ."

She paused. It was an agonisingly long pause—a pause so long, I swear I could see tumbleweed pass along the stage.

The contestants looked at each other. What was going to happen? Were we to be sent away disappointed? Or were we to be sent onwards into the unknown? Finally, with the tension ratcheted up, Simon broke the seemingly endless silence.

"You're all through to the live finals. Congratulations!"

As the other contestants cheered and hugged each other, I stood there, not quite believing it. I was gobsmacked. This journey that had started with a flipped coin at home was now about to get more serious and more daunting: I was going to be singing live on national television in front of an audience of millions.

Preparations for the live shows started soon after. I went back to London to decide on the repertoire I would work on for the semi-final and final. I'd been asked to provide five options, so I put down five different arias, including "Che Gelida Manina," "E Lucevan le Stelle," and "Nessun Dorma."

I had a meeting with one of the producers to discuss the options. The producer felt my list was too full-on operatic; he felt I should consider something a bit more well known and popular. He suggested Andrea Bocelli's "Time to Say Goodbye" and "You Raise Me Up," made famous in the UK by Irish boyband Westlife, as well as "Nessun Dorma." I took his suggestions onboard and agreed to add them to my set-list, though I preferred "Nessun Dorma" to "You Raise Me Up." I started learning the songs in the way I always did, by listening to them repeatedly on the music player of my mobile phone. Within a few days I was familiar with them.

The next stage was meeting up with the vocal coach for the shows. Her name was Yvie Burnett, a pretty blonde with a beautiful Scottish accent. To my joy, she was a trained opera singer, a mezzo-soprano, and we quickly became good friends. We had a session or two in London, and to bring the rehearsals closer to some contestants, some further ones in Birmingham. The biggest struggle for me was the verses for "Time to Say Goodbye." The chorus was sustained and very easy to remember, but the verses required pacing and flexibility. Yvie and I worked hard on this, and I surprised myself with how quickly I was able to get around the difficulties I was having.

I had another session with Yvie and a choreographer at Birmingham's Custard Factory studios. When they mentioned having a choreographer in I was startled, as I hoped they weren't going to ask me to dance, too. I knew I was hopeless at dancing!

The remaining acts also had meetings with industry lawyers, to go through the contracts involved in appearing on the show. There was the possibility that Simon might activate some of the recording contracts we were being asked to sign. One of the other acts felt we weren't getting a great deal, and suggested that we threaten to withdraw from the competition in order to get a better offer. I remember shaking my head in disbelief. Here we were, with an opportunity to perform in front of millions, and some were prepared to risk throwing it all away. I had no experience with contracts and royalties, but common sense told me that refusing our services would be fruitless. Adam, our appointed solicitor (whom we had voted for in a majority vote), told us that the contract on the table was a standard Sony contract, and in fact one of the better ones in the industry.

I felt I had to speak up. "Think about it," I said. "This isn't just a singing show. It's not a matter of having just a few reserves; they have to cover for the balance of talents. I'm betting that they have a reserve for every one of us."

Adam confirmed this was the case. Eventually, everyone agreed to go ahead with the contracts.

The live shows were scheduled for June, and ITV asked us to take two weeks out of our schedules and work commitments. I was granted this time off from work with no difficulty. In fact, Carphone Warehouse had been helpful about the competition throughout: they'd let me switch roles from managing Port Talbot to being a team leader at their Bridgend outlet, in order to give me time to prepare for the show.

It turned out that we weren't needed for the first week, so I spent that time hiking in the Lake District. Walking had become a big passion of mine over the years. I'd started hiking seriously with my brother Tony shortly after I'd started working for Tesco. We'd walked the West Highland Way in Scotland, and even walked from John O'Groats to Land's End in aid of the charity Mencap. Ever since, I've always taken the opportunity to walk whenever I can.

The week in the Lake District was spent getting fresh air and doing phone interviews with journalists. I remember doing one with Karen Price from *Wales on Sunday* at the base of Nab Scar, just at the start of a thirty-mile walk over Fairfield, Dollywagon Pike, and Helvellyn. That wasn't the only long walk I did that week. One of my regular ones started in Ambleside, climbed

Loughrigg Fell, and encompassed the full length of Great Langdale before climbing Rossett Pike. I particularly liked the view from the top of Rossett Ghyll. It was a tough climb, but the view over the valley and the distant pastureland took my breath away almost as much as the climb had! Then I passed Angle Tarn and continued to the Scafell Massif via Great End, totaling over thirty-five miles with over six thousand feet of ascent. It was dark by the time I arrived back in Ambleside. I had a well-earned pint of good bitter at the Old Dungeon Ghyll Hotel at the end of that!

As I headed south to London, I got a call from the head of media at ITV. She told me that my audition had been shown to the media as part of the screening of the very first episode of *Britain's Got Talent*.

"Your audition went down really well," she said. "There were very hard-nosed journalists in that room who were reduced to tears." I didn't know what was ahead of me, so this left me feeling hopeful but confused. I'd just stood in front of the judges for three minutes—I didn't really understand how that could make people react like this.

I was staying with some of the other acts in the North London district of Cricklewood, at a smart hotel called the Crown. On arrival we were given a briefing by Ollie and Jenna, the researchers who were looking after us. They were great, and both really hard working; they always seemed to be on hand. Initially, I was very nervous about being around the other acts, as we were effectively competing against each other. But I needn't have worried: we all got on like a house on fire, and sat together in the upstairs bar to watch each other's performances.

There was a core group of us that met for dinner and to watch each evening's programmes: Bessie Cursons and her parents, who were from my old holiday haunt of Portsmouth; the puppeteer Damon Scott, who seemed to be very confident; and Mike Garbutt, an impersonator whose attitude was very similar to mine. He was a nice guy who struggled a little for confidence, but was very good at what he did.

One of the brightest stars in the room was little Connie Talbot. She was a pretty little girl who seemed very mature for her tender six years. The common thought amongst the adult competitors was that she was the most likely winner. Connie was self-assured without being overconfident, and had just the right kind of cuteness without its feeling forced and sickly sweet. I got on well with her parents, who seemed very down-to-earth and pleasant.

My audition was shown on Saturday, 9 June as part of the first-ever show of *Britain's Got Talent*. I wasn't sure whether I wanted to watch it or not, but I managed to get through it, and was congratulated by everyone else in the room. Several of them told me that I had a good chance of winning. I did my best to put aside what they were saying; I was nervous enough without the extra pressure of hoping to win.

One thing we were all unprepared for was the amount of interest there was from the media, and in particular from the newspapers. I think it also took ITV's press office by surprise, as before long we were getting called directly, although they did check with ITV beforehand as to whether it was okay.

The calls started with a few requests being passed through Jenna and Ollie and one or two face-to-face interviews, complete with photographs. Then it just snowballed from there. Although

I had dealt with the press before in my role as a city councillor in Bristol, that was local press only. Dealing with the likes of the *Daily Mail*, the *Mirror*, and the *Sun* was a different animal altogether.

Through Jenna, I also got calls with offers to fix my teeth. This was something I had always considered, as I hated the way they looked. This felt like a real bonus, and Jenna took the dentists' details. I didn't know what else the week would hold, and I did my best to keep my expectation levels low. Having low confidence really helped with this. I never believed that anyone would pick me, so merely being at the live rounds felt like the FA Cup Final for me.

Meanwhile, there were more sessions with Yvie as I went through "Time to Say Goodbye" a few more times. The producers decided that if I made it to the final, then I would perform "Nessun Dorma" again. So in case I did make it, we also went through that as well.

The Thursday of the semi-final came all too quickly. It was a fairly warm day. I had been fitted for a tuxedo for the performances on the show, but dressed casually for the rehearsals. I didn't realize the rehearsals were going to be shown in the video introduction before my entrance, and I remember thinking how scruffy I looked! The rehearsal took place in the same studio that the live show would be broadcast from later. There were lots of people milling around and three substitutes standing in for Piers, Amanda, and Simon.

After a full run-through, I recorded a short piece to introduce myself for the video that would precede my performance. The producers wanted me to talk about my lack of confidence. They felt that if I told the audience why I felt this way, then viewers would be more likely to vote for me. There was a lot more that I *could* tell them: there was the bullying at school, which I had talked very briefly and generally about. Then there was also the abuse at the hands of Burton-Barri. Would I use this to help me win? I felt sure the producers would love to hear about it.

I decided to talk a little about how the bullying made me feel, but that I wasn't going to say anything about the abuse. If I spoke about it, I'd never know whether I had gone further or even won *because* of the abuse, rather than in spite of it. I would never know, and ultimately I'd be giving the effects of the abuse even more control over me. It would mean that I could never rely on any success being solely due to my voice. So I kept that information to myself.

By now, the clock was ticking until we were live on air. The acts for that night's show were given a briefing by the judges. Originally it was planned that the X's—the judges' buttons to vote acts offstage—would not be used for the live shows. However, due to the competition between *Britain's Got Talent* and rival shows such as BBC1's *The Apprentice* and Channel 4's *Big Brother*, it was decided that the X's would reappear after all.

This was a very unwelcome update, and added to the already nervous feeling around Fountain Studios in Wembley. Several of the other contestants assured me there was no way I would get buzzed, but I couldn't be sure, so I tried not to think about it. It was a dramatic end to the preparations for the first semi-final, which was the last thing I wanted or needed. I just wanted to get it over and done with.

SUCCESS

There were eight acts performing in the semi-final, and it was decided that I would perform last. To some of the contestants it seemed like an advantage to be on last, but not for me. It meant I had more time to think about things—more time to get nervous, to lose all courage, to forget the words. I worried that the waiting would be too much for me, and that in front of millions of people, my mind would go blank. I feared opening my mouth and nothing coming out. In my dressing room, I tried to occupy myself until call time by listening to my performance music on my phone. This didn't seem to help much at all, so I listened to different music. If the words weren't in my mind by now, they never would be.

By the time I got the call I was in a complete haze. I made my way down the stairs and along the corridor to the backstage area. The other acts, who were now waiting for the end of the show, wished me good luck. I stood and waited for my turn, which seemed to come too soon. Standing behind two huge video walls acting as doors, I could hear my voice on the video clip being shown, ending with the words "I'm somebody. I'm Paul Potts."

The doors opened. Part of me was excited, but part of me wanted to get it over and done with. I walked forwards to the microphone. The music started, and it was time to begin. Thankfully, there were no hitches, no forgotten words. I managed to find that place I went to when I sang—the one where I was in a different world. As I finished singing "Time to Say Goodbye," a shower of pyrotechnics rained down behind me.

As with the initial audition, there was a huge reaction to my performance from inside the auditorium. I was relieved that it had seemed to go well, particularly as the judges had not been slow in buzzing some of the other acts. As the audience's cheers subsided, the judges started to speak. They were all really complimentary: Amanda spoke about the death of her father, something she had not talked about before the show, and that he would have voted for me. Piers talked about his reaction to my voice.

Now it was Simon's turn to speak. *Please be nice*, I pleaded inwardly. At that moment I realised that, contrary to the instructions of the stage manager, I had left my mobile phone in my trouser pocket. Someone was calling me. I could feel the phone vibrating, and prayed I had put it on silent.

My phone was normally set to vibrate, then ring at maximum volume. And not just to any old ringtone either. I had been an avid watcher of the TV drama series *Life on Mars*, and had downloaded an amusing ringtone voiced by Philip Glenister in the character of a 1970s police inspector. The ringtone was set to say "Oi! Fatty! Shut it, and have another pie!"

Waiting for Simon to speak were the longest seconds of my life so far. If my phone wasn't on silent, I felt sure that it would be the end of any hopes of a career. Thankfully, when Simon started speaking, my phone subsided.

"Every time you come on, I want you to do well," Simon said. "And you just did again. It was magic."

I was hugely relieved, twice over. When I got offstage, I told the crew about my phone. At this revelation, they shook their heads:

"Don't do it again, Paul," the stage manager said, trying, and failing, to stop himself laughing out loud.

Now it was time to wait for the results. There was a very short gap while the phone lines were open, and then the votes were counted. I didn't want to think about the result. I thought I had sung okay, although I didn't feel I'd done my best. It was too late to do anything about it now, though; I just had to wait for the viewers' decision.

The results were in. The acts were led out on the stage, and we were put into our allotted positions. When I watched television at home, I always felt the urge to shout at the screen when hosts held on before announcing the winner. "Get on with it, for God's sake!" I'd yell. Standing there on stage, I was thinking exactly that as Ant and Dec started announcing the results. Finally, the preamble was over.

"The first act," Ant announced, "going through to the final of *Britain's Got Talent* is . . ."

". . . Paul Potts!"

I felt a rush of relief wash over me. I cupped my hands over my mouth. I'd made it through to the final!

For the first time in a long while, I was feeling successful. However, this emotion was tinged with sadness. That wasn't only for Amanda Holden, who had lost her father, but also because one of Julz's favourite aunts had lost her long fight against cancer the previous week. Aunt Sheila had made our wedding cake, and I'll always remember her lying on the floor in front of me, with a rose in her teeth, as I sang Robbie Williams's "Angels" at our wedding reception. Julz's side of the family have always been a laugh a minute; being a large family, they're a bit like a travelling show. This was Aunt Sheila's way of messing around.

There wasn't much time between the semi-final and the final: just three days. I had plenty of rehearsals to keep my mind off things, and also the introduction to my spot on the final to record. The location the crew chose for that was a little crazy; they wanted me to walk to and beyond the camera on a very crowded Oxford Street at lunchtime. What should have taken just a few minutes ended up taking three hours, as I was repeatedly stopped by passersby who wanted to congratulate me. It felt strange yet touching to have people I didn't know giving me encouragement.

That was just one sign of the impact the programme was having. The media were now taking a real interest, and not just in the UK but all over the world: the first audition seemed to have made a splash everywhere, and I was being interviewed by journalists from Australia to South Africa and the United States. It was really quite bewildering. I spent much of my time in the hotel lobby taking calls from journalists on my mobile.

At first, the media interest was very positive and supportive. But as the final neared, it started to become more cynical. I had one call from the *Sun* newspaper accusing me of misleading the public and suggesting that I was already a professional. I explained that while I'd had some coaching, it had been years earlier, and that one master class with Pavarotti didn't amount to being trained by him. I told the journalist that I had supplied all of this information to the programme, and it was there for everyone to see on the *Britain's Got Talent* website. I had never made any money from my singing before, so I felt justified in saying I was an amateur.

Many other interviews went in a similar way. While I did feel a little embattled, I knew that if I refused to answer the questions, the newspapers would add two and two together and come up with whatever number they wanted. I remained polite but firm about my history of singing and held my ground. In many ways, this was the first time I had ever really stood up for myself without losing my temper.

The nastiest interview was yet to come. In spring 2007, a young girl named Madeleine McCann had gone missing from the accommodation in Portugal where she was staying with her parents. It was, and still is, big news. As the final approached, I had not one, not two, but three calls from a reporter with the *Daily Star Sunday*. The call didn't start well. He began by asking what I thought my chances were of winning the competition. The journalist was attempting to get me to say I was a sure thing when I knew full well that I wasn't. He asked me what I thought of the sweetheart of a little girl, Connie Talbot. I told him that she was as bright as a button, and her maturity belied her young years.

"Do you think she will win," the reporter asked, "because she looks like Madeleine McCann?"

I was horrified. How could anyone be so incredibly insensitive and nasty? Worse still, I felt I knew exactly what he was trying to do. It seemed he was trying to entrap me into giving them a headline that might read "Paul Potts says Connie will win because she looks like missing girl, Madeleine McCann."

The journalist phoned me three times, and on each occasion asked me the same question. I made a point of telling Jenna, who looked after both Connie and me and let the other contestants know as well. It turned out that I wasn't the only one this journalist had tried to entrap; he'd tried the same trick on some of the others, too. I sat down with Connie's parents, explaining what had been happening, and also to warn them in case the subject was raised with them.

I felt there was a very real risk the reporter would try to suggest that, despite our denials, one of us had said yes to his question. When he rang me for the third time and once more asked about Connie, I was extremely firm with him.

"Listen," I told him, "I have refused to answer that for the last two days. It is a blatant attempt to cause mischief. What makes you think I will be stupid enough to justify your spiteful question with an answer?"

That was the only time I have ever had to hang up on a call from a journalist. I was furious that he would be so nasty, and that he was trying to kill any hope that I might just get some success after the show. It was quite the revelation for me. I was fighting for something for myself, for a change, rather than lying down and allowing someone to walk all over me.

Dealing with journalists wasn't the only thing I had to get used to. I also met the people who were to become my managers after the show. Richard Griffiths and Harry Magee told me that not only were they going to be looking after me, but that there was already considerable interest from several record companies. They came across a bit like "good cop–bad cop," Harry being the gentler one and Richard the firm one. I've since learned this to be true. They were, and are, a great double act and perfect foils for each other. The whole situation was difficult to get my head around; for years, no one had seemed interested, yet following a coin toss and two performances, my life was now doing an about-turn.

All of this put added pressure on me to succeed. I didn't dare to believe it too much, though, because I knew that once there was expectation, it would play on my nerves. So far I had kept my jitters in check by having no expectations at all. Having nothing to lose helped me not think about what was happening. For all Richard and Harry's talk about record companies, I needed to maintain that feeling and keep my expectation levels down. As the final approached, I genuinely thought little Connie Talbot would win the show. That, too, was the thinking amongst the other finalists.

In the final rehearsals, I went through "Nessun Dorma" a few more times. By the end, I really felt I had sung it well. So well, I worried whether or not I could replicate it on the night. In addition to the singing, the producers also wanted to rehearse talking with the presenters. I made a conscious decision that I didn't want to say in an interview with Ant and Dec what I would actually say in the final itself.

From always being on the sidelines and from studying media as part of my degree, I had learned to read body language and to judge people's intentions from their eyes. I had watched shows like *Britain's Got Talent* before, and recognised the expression on people's faces that made it look like they were reading something: they were recollecting what they'd said before. I didn't want to rehearse what I would actually say, as I didn't want it to come across as practised and therefore insincere. It is how I have continued to handle interviews ever since.

I had a very nervous wait after rehearsals for stage time, and eventually we were called down. When we were taken to our holding room, Amanda Holden was there having her makeup done. It was great that she wanted to spend time with us all before we went on stage. We got a real sense that she had been in that situation before, and knew how we were all feeling.

It was little Connie who broke the silence first. "I'm going to make you cry again, tonight, Amanda!" she said.

Everybody laughed, and no one doubted that she was right. Yvie was there, and came over to speak to each of us individually. When it was my turn, she came over and whispered in my ear. "Paul! Your flies are undone!"

I was hugely grateful for her spotting that. Thanks to Yvie, I wasn't after all going to be walking out in front of fourteen million people with my trousers unzipped. I'd learned my lesson from the semi-final, too, and made a point of making sure that my mobile phone was safely locked away in my dressing room.

There were five other acts in the final: dance group Kombat Breakers, Connie Talbot, Bessie Cursons, jugglers the Bar Wizards, and Damon Scott. Once again, I was chosen to perform last. Once again, the time soon came for me to enter the stage. Although I had performed "Nessun Dorma" at the start of competition, singing it again felt anything other than easy.

I was aware that at the start, any success was unexpected, whereas now expectations were raised, and this increased the pressure on me. So much so that I could feel my legs beginning to shake while I was waiting for the doors at the back of the stage to open. I found I was checking the words of "Nessun Dorma" under my breath, and I told myself to shut up. It was too late to think about that now.

"He's our final act of the night," Dec announced. "It's Paul Potts!"

The doors opened, and to cheers from the audience I walked out through the dry-ice fog effect to the microphone. I gave a wave to the crowd and then the very short introduction started. I felt my knees trembling and the nerves still trying to take control of my body. The tension I'd lost during the rehearsals had returned with a vengeance. I could feel the tension in my neck, signaled by a tightness across the back, and knew this would affect my tone, making it tighter and thinner.

To me, for all the applause from the audience at the end of the song, I had given an unsatisfactory performance. Tension had been my enemy, and I felt sure this was the end of the road. At least I made it this far—that's a real achievement, I thought to myself. I was resigned to defeat when Ant and Dec came across. I appreciated the lift in confidence the show had given me, and wanted to express this in the interview.

"I don't believe in all honesty that this has happened to me," I told them. "It's so difficult to believe, and I'm just so grateful that I'm able to gain a bit of confidence. I should have more faith in myself, and I'm working on that. It's really shown me the way."

It was time for the judges' comments. Piers began, recalling my original audition back in Wales.

"I remember you coming on stage in that terrible suit," he said. "The expectation level was very low. I turned to Simon and we both raised our eyebrows when you said 'opera.' And then you began to sing . . . when you finished that audition, I remember thinking, I have just seen the winner of *Britain's Got Talent* . . . having watched you perform again, that same song, I still think we have seen the winner of *Britain's Got Talent*."

"You won't be going back to Carphone Warehouse," Amanda

went next, to cheers from the audience. "You won't be on any kind of pay-as-you-go. You'll be on a contract from Monday."

"Your story touched everyone when you came out," Simon spoke last. "A shy, humble man with an extraordinary talent. I want to give the underdog a shot on this show, and I'd love you to win after that performance."

These comments were heartening, but I knew it was the public vote that would matter most, and who would decide the winner. I'd felt the judges' comments would be made irrelevant by my not getting enough votes to win, due to my performance. I didn't feel worthy of the comments, so inwardly brushed them aside. The finalists had to wait a very long hour before the result would be announced. It was the longest hour of my life! I went to the canteen, but I couldn't eat a thing. In the end, I decided I didn't want to be around other people, so I went to the dressing room and had some time to myself.

After what seemed like an eternity, we were called down to the holding area to return to the stage. It was results time. I was asked to look after Connie, as we would be entering from the same set of stairs, me after her. I just prayed that, bearing in mind my clumsiness, I wouldn't trip and fall down the steps.

Ant and Dec called our names one by one, and we walked out to our allotted spaces on stage. We stood all in one line, and Ant and Dec recapped what the judges had said about our performances.

"And this is it," Dec said to a hushed silence from the audience. "The winner . . . of *Britain's Got Talent* . . . is . . ."

SUCCESS

The wait for the announcement was agony. My heart felt like it had stopped. The audience were cheering and shouting out the names of who they wanted to win. Please, I thought, just shout out a name, any name—just let the agony be over!

And then my life changed forever.

CHAPTER THIRTEEN

On Record

". . . PAUL POTTS!"

In my disbelief, I exclaimed into my cupped hands, "How the hell did this happen?" I felt a sense of elation and disbelief rush over me. I had won! The studio audience were on their feet, cheering and applauding. Ant and Dec tried to interview me, but the noise was so loud I couldn't hear what I was saying. Then, as the judges offered me their congratulations—Piers: "You've earned it. You deserve it." Amanda: "God, well done and good luck with the rest of your life; it's going to be fabulous!"—Simon took my breath away. "Paul, I am so proud of you, and I want to say something very quickly. Next week you are going to be in a recording studio, making your debut album."

I couldn't believe it. Here I was, a thirty-six-year-old over-weight man with dodgy teeth, and Simon was telling me this. Was I dreaming?

It was time to give my winner's performance. For the first

time in the final I felt relaxed, and to me the performance felt like the best of the whole series.

It was the start of a crazy night. Afterwards, I was reunited with Julz, and we were both taken to the ITV2 studio to speak with Stephen Mulhern. After a fun interview, as interviews with Stephen always are, we headed back to the bar area and had a few drinks. The whole family was there, but after a while I went back up to my dressing room. I just needed to get my own space for a few seconds, to pause and take stock of what had just happened. It still hadn't sunk in.

By the time I came back down a lot of the crowd had gone, and we all headed back to my hotel. The bar was still open, and with the little money I had remaining I bought a round of drinks. I was pretty much skint after the evening, but for once I had a devil-may-care attitude. I had just won £100,000, so surely things would now be a bit easier. It was a great night, though I was aware that Julz and I had an interview to do in the morning with breakfast television show *GMTV*. We had to be up at five to get in the car at five thirty to head to the studios on the South Bank. Before we knew it, it was four in the morning and we were still up! Julz fell asleep as soon as we reached our room; it seemed that in no time the alarm went off.

The next few days were a blur. I had a never-ending round of interviews and photographs to do, plus my very first press conference. This was a very new experience for me, and it became immediately apparent that I would need to adapt or else become overwhelmed. It was very daunting, and I felt a little besieged; it was difficult to stay grounded and avoid being swept up in the moment. Just as I had not allowed the negative things that had happened in my life to affect who I was, I couldn't allow this upturn in my circumstances to change me, either.

While I was busy with all this in London, Julz returned to Wales. I needed her to post my passport, as I discovered I was flying to New York, and also we needed to speak to our bank. Despite having just won £100,000, we were down to only a few pounds and needed to arrange an overdraft to see us through the next few weeks. The bank refused the request, even being rude to Julz in person when she went into the Port Talbot branch of Barclays. I vowed that once the winning money arrived we would change our bankers.

On Tuesday morning, I flew to New York. It was the first time I had ever travelled business class, and I couldn't believe it. There appeared to be acres of space in my seat, and a great pair of headphones to watch the in-flight movie. When we arrived, we went to a store where they altered a suit for me to wear the next day. I was to perform "Nessun Dorma" at Rockefeller Plaza, live on NBC's *Today Show*, which was a huge honour.

I toured the city with a journalist and photographer for *News of the World*. As we made our way round, we were followed by a crowd of paparazzi, which I found funny. They would poke their heads out from behind a building, a camera flash would fire, and then they would dart away again. It was a long, tiring day, and after a shoot round Times Square and dinner, it was well after midnight before I got back to my hotel. It was after two in the morning when I fell asleep fully clothed on the bed, having forgotten to set an alarm.

* * *

New York is a bustling place, and one of my favourite cities in the world. It was on this trip that I discovered this buzzing city with a real heartbeat. I saw lots of things in a short period of time: Times Square, Central Park—and we went to the top of the Rockefeller Center, the famous Top of the Rock, with the most amazing view over the city.

Once again, I had an early start. I had to be up at four thirty for a five thirty sound check on Rockefeller Plaza. Thankfully, my body clock was aware, and I awoke at exactly the right time. I showered, changed into fresh clothes, and strolled across to the plaza. I was overawed that I was playing on the same stage that one of Julz's heroes, Bon Jovi, had performed on only a few days before. It was a crisp and sunny June morning and there was a great atmosphere in the area. Lots of people had turned out to watch. I got to meet some of them, shake their hands, and for the first time, sign autographs.

For an outside area, the acoustics were great. The tall buildings surrounding us channelled the sound around the area. It felt surreal, singing in New York and being watched by millions of Americans across the country. But it also felt blissful to be standing there doing what I loved doing. Was I dreaming? I didn't know. All I did know was that it felt great, and if it was a dream, I didn't want to wake up.

Simon Cowell was true to his word about the album recording. While I was in New York, I was given a personal CD player along with a CD of suggested songs for the record: these included Italian-language versions of "Everybody Hurts" and Ennio Morricone's "Nella Fantasia." I listened to it to get a feeling for the material, though didn't have much time. I was booked into a studio back in London on the Sunday, a week after the final, as Simon had promised.

I returned to London and was put up in the Conrad Hotel in Chelsea Harbour. This was to be my home for the next seven weeks, on and off. It was an all-suite hotel, beyond five-star and beyond what I was used to. I had come to the point where I needed some laundry doing, and when I looked at the price of washing, my eyes almost popped out of their sockets. Five pounds to wash a pair of underpants? Ten pounds to wash a T-shirt? I didn't have a T-shirt with me that cost that much! In fact, the one I was looking to put in only cost me two pounds!

I worked with three different producers on my debut record, *One Chance*. There was Nigel Wright, whom I had worked with on *Britain's Got Talent*, and also two Swedish double acts: Per Magnusson and David Kreuger, who have also worked with artists such as Leona Lewis, Josh Groban, and Celine Dion; and Andreas "Quiz" Romdhane and Josef Larossi, known as Quizlarossi, who had worked with Il Divo, Kelly Clarkson, and Diana Ross. I didn't have a lot of time to get to know them, as it was very intense.

Recording an album was an alien idea to me, and although I had been in a radio station before, this was the first time I had been in a recording studio. To me, the mixing desk looked like the controls for a spaceship. I didn't know how things were normally done in recording sessions and knew that as a newcomer, especially one untried and untested, I was very much the junior partner in the whole process. I had learned in life to pick my battles carefully, and apart from asking for sheet music rather than just lyric sheets, I didn't push for too much.

SUCCESS

The different producers had different ways of going about things. I wasn't sure about the repetitive style of recording everything line by line preferred by the Swedish producers. To me it felt like I wasn't getting a proper feel of the whole piece. With Nigel, I had a chance to record the whole piece in a single take, stopping only later to pick up individual phrases to polish. Nigel's approach felt more natural and also more classical. However, I knew that until I proved myself, I would have to go along with others' ways of working. In later recordings, I changed my recording style to singing passes of the whole piece, going back later to pick up individual phrases as necessary.

The days were long; my first day's recording took over fourteen hours, with only a few breaks for refreshment and lunch. Some of the backing tracks were already recorded, and some tracks I recorded first with the orchestra and then immediately after to the orchestral recording. The next day I told Yvie that despite my lack of formal training, I must have some technique, as otherwise I was sure I would not be able to talk, let alone sing! I wanted to do as well as I could, bearing in mind the time restrictions and the fact I was new to the business and learning my way.

There was no time to lose: the final of *Britain's Got Talent* had been on 17 June, and the album was due for release on 16 July. We recorded the main part of the album in just eight days. I was happy overall with the results, and was particularly happy with "Nessun Dorma," which needed only a few takes to get done to both mine and the producer's satisfaction. It was a strange feeling when I got my hands on a finished copy—again, I had to pinch myself to prove this was really happening.

Shortly before the album's release, I returned to Wales for my first public performance in the UK since winning. Another classical singer local to the area, Katherine Jenkins, was performing Katherine in the Park at Port Talbot's Margam Castle, and I was invited to perform "Nessun Dorma."

The following week, *One Chance* was released. It went straight in at number one, selling over 128,000 copies and going gold immediately. The record outsold the rest of the top ten put together, and would stay at the top of the charts for three weeks. It would go on to hit number one round the world, including Ireland, Australia, New Zealand, Denmark, Norway, Sweden, and South Korea. I was amazed and humbled that so many people had bought my album. It seemed very strange that only a few weeks before, I was serving people in Carphone Warehouse, but now they were actually buying my album!

The pace of those first few weeks after winning *Britain's Got Talent* didn't let up. Even when I had time off, I still found myself singing and performing. I discovered that Quex Park in Margate, where I had performed as a guest with the Royal Philharmonic Concert Orchestra, was hosting another concert in aid of the Cancer Care charity at Margate's Queen Elizabeth The Queen Mother Hospital. Remembering the promise I had made in 1999, I called Albie Park and offered my services free of charge in aid of the charity. Albie was delighted that I'd remembered, and I returned to perform on another beautiful Kent evening.

I had a trip to Hamburg, which was the first of many to Germany. I met people who would become friends: Dave "Shacky" Shackleton, vice president of Sony UK's international department, and Vivian Hauner, the head of TV promotion for Sony Music in Germany. Since I had studied German at school, I did my best to speak as much German as I could remember from my lessons twenty years earlier. It was a short visit, as I needed to return to the studio to record some Christmas songs for the US edition of the album, and also a special Christmas edition of the record for release elsewhere.

During the recording of this extra material, and perhaps not surprisingly given my schedule, I developed a cold. The show, though, had to go on, and I was fighting a sore throat as I flew to Prague to record a music video at the State Opera House. Again I sang for over twelve hours. Normally, music videos are partly lip-synced and partly "sung out"—although the sound is never actually recorded. I had asked about only lip-syncing, despite the recording being in a major opera house, and misunderstood the request to only sing out the closeups, and instead sang all the way through. The lights were hot and bright, and at times I felt sure I knew what a spit roast felt like!

We'd had a very early start, leaving the hotel at seven and not arriving back until after two the following morning. Far from getting any rest, I had to be up again in a few hours to travel to Norway. I was due to perform in Oslo on the shores of the Oslo Fjord, and then onwards to Stockholm for more recording. In Norway, I felt something was not quite right with my voice during my performance of "Nessun Dorma." The following morning my throat was getting scratchy, although it wasn't painful, but after spending a little time recording in Stockholm I could feel it was going completely.

I woke up the following morning, barely able to speak at all.

This was a very bad time to lose my voice: I had a concert in Carlisle and also trips to the other side of the world to come. I went to see an ENT specialist, who prescribed antibiotics and a small dose of oral steroids to help bring the inflammation down. But even so, I had to withdraw from the concert in Carlisle and from promotion trips to Amsterdam and Copenhagen.

Even though I couldn't sing, the promoters asked me to go to Carlisle, as they were worried they'd be accused of misleading the public if I wasn't there. Carlisle Live was an all-day concert, headlined by Westlife, with a star-studded lineup playing to twenty thousand fans. I travelled up in a private jet, something I had never experienced before. I was surprised by how small it was and how luxurious it *wasn't*. It was designed for convenience, not comfort. The one advantage was that the pilot negotiated a gentle take off and approach to help with the pressure imbalance in my ears. I flew with the other acts, amongst them the friendly Shayne Ward and the very chatty Louis Walsh, Westlife manager and *X Factor* judge. Louis was interesting, but relentless. He had a lot of views on the business and what I should record in the future. Some I agreed with; others I didn't.

I had been told to stay quiet, and that if I wanted to say something, to speak up rather than whisper (whispering forces air through the vocal cords, so it tires them quicker). I went onstage and explained in very croaky tones that I was unable to perform due to losing my voice. The audience understood, and I made my way over to meet those who'd paid for VIP access tickets. Bearing in mind that I was ill, I was offered the opportunity to go to the large house, which served as the artists' private area, but I felt that as I was being paid a fee, I should make myself available for as long as possible. It was clear that I needed a break.

I had a couple of weeks' complete voice rest—which Julz described as bliss!—and she and I spent a few days at a health spa just outside the Somerset town of Shepton Mallet. I spent a good deal of time in the mentholated steam room and, along with medication, this seemed to help make progress. I had a massage, which helped me to relax, and Julz also had a few treatments while we were there. I checked in with the ENT specialist, who had a look down my throat using a small camera. He confirmed that progress was being made and that I would be able to travel abroad as planned.

The promotional work now took me all round the world: from the Far East back to Europe, and then on to North America. It was by far my longest trip abroad, and I was pleased that accompanying me were Julz and one of the marketing managers at Sony International UK, Paul Kindred. I liked Paul a lot; we became friends, and there was always a good bit of banter between us.

Our first stop was Hong Kong. To my amazement, a round-the-world ticket in first class turned out to be cheaper than a ticket in business class, so our flight out to Hong Kong was very luxurious indeed. It started with caviar and salmon served with champagne, and Julz and I slept well in spacious seats wide enough for the two of us to sit in one together.

We arrived well rested in Hong Kong, where I performed at a very busy press conference. My voice was still recovering and I was nowhere near my best, but there was no choice but to try as hard as possible while taking as much care as I could. As well as a shortened performance, there were scores of interviews to do with TV crews from all across Asia, including journalists from Korea, Japan, Malaysia, and China. From Hong Kong we flew on to New Zealand. Never having been as far afield as this before, I thought Auckland was just a short trip from Hong Kong, perhaps five hours. After all, it didn't look all *that* far on a globe. I was wrong—it was another fourteen hours. Our destination, however, made up for the journey; we stayed at a beautiful boutique hotel called Mollie's, close to Auckland's harbour.

It took a while to adjust to the new time zone. Julz and I had been advised to stay up for as long as we possibly could, but when we sat down for dinner at eight, I felt a strange sensation, like my feet were suspended on thin air. It was jet lag. I just about finished my meal before heading straight to bed. As well as the jet lag, I got confused about what time it was back home. I called Yvie to chat about my voice and sent her into a panic. Her mum was in hospital and she'd feared the call was from there. I thought it was ten at night at home, but I'd got my sums wrong—it was one in the morning! I apologised and waited for a better time.

Bit by bit, my voice was regaining its strength, and after an all-too-short time in New Zealand we left for Sydney for my first visit to Australia. I enjoyed being down under. Life seemed to have a different pace, and everyone was very friendly and welcoming. Views over the harbour from our hotel, the Intercontinental, were stunning, particularly at night. The view from the roof garden was hard to beat.

I did a number of TV appearances in Sydney, where the sights were wonderful, the sun sparkling on the water and ships and boats of all sizes passing across the harbour. One of my TV appearances included the city's iconic opera house. I was told on camera that I would be performing there as part of an Australian tour the following year. That took my breath away. To be honest, I hadn't thought that far ahead; I hadn't even resigned from my job at Carphone Warehouse. But to go on a world tour and perform at Sydney Opera House felt like yet another dream I didn't want to wake up from.

After Australia, we went back to Europe the long way round, going via Los Angeles to change planes. I was due in the United States shortly, but it was worth heading back to Europe first. In Germany, I performed on *Die Johannes B. Kerner Show*, one of the biggest shows on German TV. I then went on to Denmark, to appear on its main evening news programme. That trip to Copenhagen was incredible. The TV show had expected a couple of thousand people to turn up to watch me perform in the famous and picturesque City Hall Square. By the time I got on stage, there were *twenty thousand* people there to hear me sing! I sang "Nessun Dorma" and "Con Te Partiro," and the audience response was amazing. In Sweden, my next stop, I avoided another expensive hotel laundry bill by washing a pair of trousers in the sink. Unfortunately, my passport was in the back pocket! I had to dry it on a towel rail, page by page. When I arrived in New York the following day the lady from US immigration gave me a sympathetic smile.

"Sir, you've washed this passport, haven't you?"

Everything about the American leg of my promotional tour seemed to be on a grand scale. I spent a lot of time in a studio doing interviews via satellite links. It felt a little strange to not always see someone at the other end, and really brought home to me just how large the United States is.

At the airport, I was picked up in the biggest car I had ever seen: an Escalade. I made a point of sitting behind the passenger seat, knowing that this would mean I'd be able to open my own door. I found it strange to have doors opened for me; I was not completely ancient, and still capable of pulling a lever! Numerous drivers would try to beat me to the door, but I would always get out first.

There was no let-up in schedule, right from the start. After having dinner with the head of radio promotion at Columbia, I headed to a radio station very close to ground zero in downtown Manhattan. I gave an hourlong interview on a talk show after midnight, Eastern Time. It had already been a long day, and by the time the interview was over it was two in the morning and I had to be up again at five for an in-studio performance for the *Today* show.

Was it tiring? A little, but I felt there were other people doing *real* jobs who felt more tired. I was also very aware that I couldn't expect to get anything out of a singing career if I didn't first put the work in. The trip turned out to be the first of several to the US that autumn. The biggest event was yet to come—a performance on *Oprah*. Julz flew out with me, and we stayed on the shores of Lake Michigan to prepare for the show. Knowing just how big this opportunity was, I met up with Gary Wallis, who was there to help on the music side. Gary is a busy musical director and drummer, and over the years has worked with the likes of Pink Floyd, Jean Michel Jarre, and Tom Jones. Gary went through the arrangement with me. I had the first signs of a cold, so I dosed myself up with honey and lemon. Fortunately, the symptoms didn't affect my performance.

I found Oprah Winfrey to be charming, with lots of charisma. It was daunting speaking to the queen of chat shows, but Oprah put me at ease, asking me about my life before and after *Britain's Got Talent*. I gave my performance of "Nessun Dorma" and she reacted well to it, with several gasps of *"Wow!"* that made me feel like blushing. I was led from the stage after giving a short interview in which I credited Julz with helping me get this far.

After the end of the TV recording, Oprah often does interviews with the guests and their families for broadcast on her website. To Julz's horror, Oprah made a beeline to interview her. Julz is quite nervous in interviews and often prefers to be in the background, so I asked if I could join her on stage to help her out. The interview ended up being the first of many Julz and I did together. We'd interact with each other in quite a funny way: Julz would make fun of me, and I would join in. A sense of humour is important in any relationship, and we demonstrated this when both Julz and I laughed at myself.

Following the *Oprah* show, Gary Wallis got us tickets to see Genesis in concert in Chicago. Gary had played as a percussionist with Mike Rutherford in Mike and the Mechanics, and so was able to get us backstage access. I had always loved both Genesis and Phil Collins, and it was a great show with the usual humour running through it.

After the show, we went backstage and, to my delight, Phil came across to talk to me and Gary. "You know," Phil said, "I was really nervous tonight that Gary would find fault with my drumming and that you [indicating me] would find my singing out of tune." I laughed and asked him how he managed to sing and drum at the same time.

"I don't know," Phil replied. "I just do it."

It was a surreal experience to find myself standing in Genesis's dressing room having drinks and chatting with Phil, Tony Banks, Mike Rutherford, Chester Thompson the drummer, and the regular lead guitarist Daryl Stuermer. Six months before, I had been selling phones in Port Talbot. Now, here I was having drinks with some of my musical heroes. Not for the first time (or last), I felt like pinching myself.

As well as the United States, I also travelled to Canada and Mexico to perform. In Toronto, I performed at First Canadian Place, and there were thousands of people there. The reaction was huge and at the signing afterwards, I met many hundreds of them. I felt privileged to meet so many people who were buying my CDs. I went back to a steak house I'd visited on holiday a few years earlier, and later learnt that someone tried to buy the seats Julz and I had sat on!

I wanted to experience some of the life of the cities I was visiting, and difficult as this could be because of my hectic schedule, I tried to make an effort to see more than just airports, studios, and hotels. During my visit to Mexico City, Julz and I found time to visit an agave farm, where we tasted the base ingredient in tequila. We walked round some of the Aztec temples and experienced some of the culture of the area. I found the Mexican people to be both friendly and very passionate. Nearly five thousand of them turned up to watch me perform on the outskirts of Mexico City, and most of them seemed to be in the queue for the post-performance signing.

SUCCESS

"Come on, Paul," the record company guy said, "we've got to leave or you're going to miss your flight back to the UK." I looked at the queue still snaking out in front of me. "I can't," I replied. "I want to see everyone who's turned up."

I was aware that the fans most likely to be disappointed if I left would be the ones who had waited the longest. I tried to imagine how disappointed I would be in their position and, despite protests, stayed and carried on signing. My luck was in: having got through the queue, we were fortunate with the traffic and made it to the airport in good time for my flight.

It had been an exhausting few months, but I wouldn't have changed them for the world. I'd been to so many amazing places and met so many wonderful people, none of which I would ever forget. I'd been touched by the response of audiences everywhere, but now my attention turned back to Britain and a special concert I needed to prepare for. Part of the prize of winning *Britain's Got Talent* was a coveted place at that year's Royal Variety Performance. As star-studded as the lineup was, there was someone in the audience even more famous. I was going to be singing in the presence of Her Majesty the Queen.

CHAPTER FOURTEEN

On the Road

"**P**LEASE WELCOME the judging panel from *Britain's Got Talent . . .*"

It was December 2007, and I stood backstage at Liverpool's Empire Theatre, waiting to start one of the biggest performances of my life. On the other side of the curtain, I could hear the applause from the audience as Piers Morgan, Amanda Holden, and Simon Cowell walked on stage to introduce me.

"The ultimate prize for the winner of *Britain's Got Talent*," Piers began, "is a performance on this very special show. A performance before royalty on the most prestigious variety show on television . . ."

The Royal Variety Performance is one of the highlights of the year in British entertainment. The very best in comedy, music, magic, dancing, and more are invited to perform in front of royalty to raise money for Entertainment Artistes' Benevolent Fund. The first performance took place in 1912, becoming an annual event from 1921 onwards. Participants over the years have ranged from the Beatles to Rudolf Nureyev, Sir John Gielgud to Placido Domingo.

". . . after a horrendous first day's auditions," Simon continued, "where the one highlight was a dancing pig, I thought we would all get beheaded. Then a very nervous-looking mobile phone salesman shuffled onto the stage and I sighed and thought, Here we go again."

It wasn't a moment to be reminded of my nerves. On the 2007 show, I was appearing alongside the likes of Enrique Iglesias, Bon Jovi, Kanye West, Joan Rivers, and Dame Kiri Te Kanawa. To be part of such a remarkable lineup was quite a daunting prospect.

"I must admit," Piers was speaking again, "that I perhaps unfairly thought that when they were dishing out talent, he was probably at the back of the queue. And when he announced he was going to sing opera, we all cringed inside, wondering what timeless classic he was about to mangle beyond all recognition." . . .

"Mangle beyond all recognition" was exactly what I didn't want to do in front of such an audience. Just to add to the tension, two days before the show I'd had my teeth done. It took a long time and turned out to be very painful. I still didn't take very well to local anaesthetic in and round my mouth, and after more than ten injections I could still feel everything. After a couple of hours of agony, everything was complete, but it felt like I was holding soft marbles in my mouth.

I'd spent the previous forty-eight hours getting used to my new teeth: to begin with, I couldn't eat anything and had to drink through a straw. Fortunately, by the time I travelled up to

Liverpool the swelling had begun to settle down, and I started to get used to the new bridge. Even so, my new teeth didn't stop me from feeling nervous. I'd spent some time working with Yvie in the conductor's room and had completely forgotten there was a cameraman following me round the venue. I missed a note during the session and lost my composure a little—something that made me cringe when I saw it on screen for the first time in a documentary!

. . . "Then he opened his mouth," Amanda told the audience out front, "and much to all our surprise, he had the voice of an angel. I couldn't believe it. The audience erupted in spontaneous applause, and of course I burst into tears."

Yvie had helped me calm down, and that made me feel a little better. I could sense that the film crew wanted to speak to me, but I needed to compose myself and prepare for my time on stage. I was called over to meet Simon Cowell, and it was good to see him. He gave me one or two words of advice, telling me to relax and enjoy the performance, which, waiting backstage, felt easier said than done!

"Of course that was Paul Potts," Simon was speaking now, "who went on to become the deserving winner of the whole competition. Since then, it's been the most incredible success story for Paul. His first album has already sold over two million copies, and he's been number one in over fifteen countries. Britain *has* got talent. Ladies and gentlemen, I am very proud to introduce . . . Paul Potts!"

The curtain lifted, and I felt incredibly exposed. Here I was, performing not just for an international television audience and a packed auditorium of invited guests, but also in front of

Her Majesty. As the audience applauded, I walked forward to the microphone and started to sing the first of my two pieces: "Nella Fantasia." I was accompanied on this and my second piece, "Nessun Dorma," by a small ensemble of female string and wind players, as well as a full orchestra in the pit in front of me. For "Nella Fantasia" a female acrobat danced behind me; for "Nessun Dorma" I was joined by a small female choir.

I got one or two words wrong in my performance, but I did eventually settle into it, and by the end really enjoyed the experience. After the show, I took my place in the lineup next to the *Britain's Got Talent* judges and was presented to the Queen and Prince Philip. They told me they had enjoyed my performance, and Prince Philip teased Simon and the judges about how they made money from me. It was very well natured and amusing, and it was such an honour to meet them and to sing for them. Performing at the Royal Variety Performance is something very few people get the opportunity to do. It was an evening I'll always remember.

Julz and I went on to the after-show party and met a lot more people there. I got to meet Sir Bobby Robson, the former England football manager who was manager of England at the 1990 World Cup, Italia 90. It was during this tournament that "Nessun Dorma" first became really well known, thanks to the BBC's decision to use it as the theme tune for their coverage. We had a good chat, and I was left with the impression that he was one of the nicest people you could meet. Sir Bobby told me he had really enjoyed my performance and that he admired my determination.

I thought the Royal Variety Performance was the perfect event to cap a remarkable year, but there was to be one more surprise for me before 2007 was out. I was asked to go and meet Simon at his house in West London. I hadn't been told what was going to happen, but was advised to arrive smartly dressed. I met Simon and he said we were going for a ride in his Rolls-Royce Phantom. We sat in the back and had a chat, all the time with a camera there to catch every moment. As we rode, I tried to work out what was going on. Very soon I noticed we were in Westminster, which confused me even further.

"What's happening?" I asked. "Where are we going?"

"You've worked so hard over the last six months," Simon said, "that I've got a treat in store for you."

I noticed to my disbelief that the car was turning left into one of the most famous streets in the world: Downing Street. I followed Simon as he went up to knock on the most famous door in Britain: Number 10. It was answered by the prime minister, Gordon Brown. I was shown around, and I met his wife, Sarah, plus the then chancellor of the exchequer, Alistair Darling. Gordon presented me with a signed copy of his book *Courage*, and told me I was a great example of just that. I didn't feel very courageous, I told him. I had simply done what I loved doing, that was all.

Over tea, the prime minister presented me with a double-platinum disc to recognise worldwide sales of two million albums. I couldn't believe it. What a year! I started it as a store manager at Carphone Warehouse and ended it selling two million albums, reaching number one in fifteen countries, and visiting even more countries. If anyone had told me on 31 December 2006 what the next year would hold, I would never have believed them.

* * *

Shortly after recording my first album, *One Chance*, I had been asked by my managers, Richard and Harry, whether I wanted to go on tour. I'd said yes, not really knowing what it would involve. Fast forward six months, and I'd spent Christmas and New Year's listening to a playlist of music that would form my show as I travelled round the world. In early 2008, I was in rehearsal rooms in East London, close to Tower Bridge, wondering just what I was about to let myself in for.

Prior to *Britain's Got Talent*, the most shows I had ever done in a week was three, at Bath Opera and at Southgate College Opera. I looked at my touring programme and started to freak out. My schedule showed me doing fifty-five shows in six months. In the UK and North American parts of the world tour, I was averaging six shows a week.

Not only did this feel like a lot, I was also very conscious of the fact that I wasn't an amateur anymore, and I wasn't playing a part. People were paying their hard-earned money to come and watch me perform. Could I pull it off? I felt nervous and tense, and was on the point of losing my nerve. When I practised the Mario Lanza–inspired *Student Prince* medley that would become a big highlight of my tour, I really struggled with the high notes. I started to panic.

Even worse than the singing was the thought of talking to an audience every night. What would I say? I didn't want someone to come and write speeches for me, as I felt this would be insincere, but the idea of speaking to thousands of people six nights a week scared me more than the singing. I was terrified, and it showed.

In later conversations with my crew, it turned out they were concerned that I might have a breakdown. This was a real test of how adaptable I really was, a real sink-or-swim moment. The one thing I knew was that I was committed now. I had to go ahead and do my best for the people who were coming to watch me. The show, to use a famous phrase, must go on.

The tour hit the ground running with a UK leg comprised of twenty-four dates in thirty-one days. It began in the classic British seaside resort of Rhyl, on the north coast of Wales. After the rehearsals in London, we took the long drive up to nearby St. Asaph where we were staying. We then headed over to Rhyl's splendid Pavilion Theatre for a last full run through before the first show.

I had a great team of people with me to help calm my nerves. There was my conductor, Mark Agnor; my musical director, Chris Taylor; the core technical team, Mark Littlewood, who dealt with front-of-house sound, and LJ, the engineer who looked after sound on stage. I was also fortunate to have a wonderful guest artist with me on tour. Natasha Marsh was an up-and-coming Welsh soprano whose debut album *Amour* had been released the previous year. She was approachable and lovely, and a real help in guiding me through my early days of touring.

I hadn't liked the term "support act," and made the decision early on that I wanted my guest to be part of the main show. That brought its own questions. Natasha and I were to perform a duet of "Brindisi" from Verdi's *La Traviata*, and I was unsure what we should do during the piece's musical interludes. Dancing didn't seem an option: firstly, I am reliably informed by Julz that I am a terrible dancer, and secondly, Natasha is much taller than I. Either I would have to stand on tiptoes or Natasha would have to bend down, making us look like a dodgy copy of *Who Framed Roger Rabbit?*'s Roger dancing with Jessica.

In the end, I decided to be a little inventive and suggested we toast and drink champagne (actually sparkling apple juice) with our arms locked. I would then exaggerate the difference in height, which usually got a good laugh. Unfortunately, occasionally some of the "champagne" would get spilt, but I figured it was better than Tash and the other sopranos getting bruised toenails or torn ball gowns.

Meanwhile, I had worked out how to get around my concerns about talking between the music. I decided my approach to the talking would be to try and imagine that I was casually chatting to friends in a bar. Being nervous meant I tended to talk a little too much, which was quite normal for me. But talking too much was probably better than not saying anything at all.

As the UK tour began, I was frightened that people would not enjoy the singing, meaning that I would be considered a fraud. Thankfully, however, my fears were to prove unfounded. The first few shows went okay, although I wasn't especially happy with all of it. I asked Mark Littlewood to record the shows from the sound desk so that I could listen back and correct things that weren't quite right. I have always been one of my harshest critics, and I wanted to learn from the mistakes I was making.

A real critic came for the first time to one of my early dates in Cambridge. He tore the show apart, which left me feeling a little unhappy, but I was heartened by the fact that the audience seemed to enjoy it. For me, they were the most important critics of all.

I knew, however, that I was not singing at my best. I was

thinking too hard about my performance and worried that the running order was causing most of the problems. Originally, when I sat down with Gary Wallis before the tour started to discuss the order, I'd suggested the great Mexican song "Granada" at the start of the show. It was a march, and the overture for the show also began with it, so I felt it was a perfect starting piece. Gary disagreed, and because this was my first tour, I'd gone along with it.

The difficulty was that "Granada" was now coming after "Caruso," one of the most passionate songs of the first half, as well as having some of the highest and most sustained notes. Following that, "Granada" was just too tough. Because I didn't think I could do it, I was having difficulty with it technically. It was the single issue that led to my beating myself up over my entire performance.

In the end, I had bad weather to thank for making the necessary change. We'd performed in Harrogate, North Yorkshire, before heading up to Scotland for our next show in Aberdeen. High winds, however, were grounding flights, which meant that rather than flying up to join us, Natasha was forced to travel up by taxi. She was busy in Leeds doing interviews for her album, so we had gone ahead in the bus. It was a long journey, and it became clear that Natasha was going to be severely delayed getting to Aberdeen's Music Hall.

I sat down with Chris Taylor, Mark Agnor, and my tour manager, Jake, and made a very quick decision about a revised running order. I moved "Granada" right to the start of the show, because we didn't yet know when Natasha would arrive. It was originally at the very end of the first half. Ending with a long high C, I wanted to perform it early, when I was fresher. She eventually made it to the venue halfway through the show. As I was singing "Ave Maria," I spotted her standing there out of breath, so I signalled to her that I would perform one more piece before introducing her. It was a testament to her adaptability and complete lack of an "attitude" that Natasha just got on with things, even joking with the audience that she had not had time on the way up for a toilet stop.

The Aberdeen show was the one that helped me really turn the corner. Chris and I agreed that from now on I'd begin with "Granada." I became more confident and performed better as a result. That fed into the talking as well as the singing. Jake suggested I make a point of keeping in touch with local and national news, and one story I particularly focused on was that of a BBC news presenter, Jeremy Paxman, who had been bemoaning the quality of Marks and Spencer's underpants. I had spotted a children's book called *Aliens Love Underpants* and suggested to the audience that Jeremy read it, and that in any case, I had hundreds of pairs of M&S pants and they hadn't yet let me down.

I was starting to enjoy myself more and more on stage. The show's reviews improved, and that helped my confidence further. Before I knew it, I was singing the last show at Hammersmith Apollo in London. This I felt was my best performance yet, and we celebrated at the K West Hotel after the show.

While we stood at the bar, Julz pointed out a guy in the corner. He was a comedian, Matthew Horne, who had played the part of Gavin in a hugely popular BBC sitcom called *Gavin & Stacey*. I had missed it, having been abroad for most of the autumn, so I didn't recognise him at all.

Next to Julz was another famous face from the series I didn't recognise: James Corden, the co-writer of *Gavin & Stacey*, who played the part of Matthew's best friend in the series. James was holding a Tesco carrier bag and looking somewhat forlorn.

"That's all they left me!" said James, mournfully.

"What?!" Julz said, trying not to laugh and failing.

"They broke into my car, and all they've left me is my dirty laundry!"

Julz broke into hysterics at this point.

James appeared indignant: "I'm telling you that someone has broken into my car and that all they have left is my dirty underwear, and all you can do is laugh at me?"

"Sorry," said Julz, "but it's your fault for being a comedian. It was the way you said it!"

Despite his annoyance, James was a funny guy and difficult not to warm to. I don't suppose either of us could have imagined that when we met again, it would be on the set of a Hollywood film, with James playing the part of me!

With the UK part of the tour complete and my confidence up, I set off for the next set of concerts in North America.

My first date was an event at the Planet Hollywood Theater in Las Vegas, before beginning the tour proper in Seminole, Florida. Julz and I spent a few days in Vegas, taking in a few shows and playing a few small wager card games. We also took the opportunity to go and see the Hoover Dam and the Grand Canyon, flying over it in a helicopter and landing on the lower parts for a champagne picnic. It was a once-in-a-lifetime experience.

SUCCESS

Part of the US and Canadian tours would be undertaken by air, and part by tour bus. This would be my first experience of travelling and sleeping on tour buses. I enjoyed the experience and the camaraderie with the other passengers. I enjoyed all the travelling, and it was great to have Julz by my side. However, she found it tiring, as she struggled to sleep on the buses and didn't enjoy living out of a suitcase.

After performances in Seminole and Tampa, the tour made its way up the east coast of the United States, with shows in Washington, DC, New York, Ledyard, Connecticut, and Boston. At Washington, DC, I was struck by the varying ages of the audience: at the stage door, I met both an eight-year-old fan and lady who was close to her century! Performing in New York City was a huge honour, but nerve-wracking as they have a reputation for being tough. But they seemed to receive me well, which was a relief. In Atlantic City, I announced my resignation from Carphone Warehouse. Up to this point I was still technically employed by them, and I'd felt that life was just too unreal for my good luck not to be a dream.

After the Boston show, I felt a cold coming on. I tried to dose myself with vitamin C and echinacea, but they weren't having any effect. The tour continued on into Canada, and my first performance in Hamilton seemed unaffected by my symptoms. But by the time I got off the tour bus in Montreal, I was bunged up, coughing, and had a temperature. I could feel the cold starting to affect my voice and booked into the spa of one of Montreal's top hotels to use their steam room. This helped clear some of it, but even so, I was feeling very rough.

I was due to play at the prestigious Place des Arts in Montreal. Postponing the concert was considered, but knowing the rivalry between Quebec and Ontario, I knew that if I cancelled the Montreal show, then I would be under pressure to do the same in Toronto and Ottawa. I made the decision to go ahead, but shortened my performance slightly. I didn't want to sing anything that might do harm to my voice, so I made the reluctant decision to cut down the *Student Prince* medley and left out "Nessun Dorma."

I was gutted because both Place des Arts in Montreal and Roy Thomson Hall in Toronto were stunning venues to perform, and I knew that I wasn't at my best in either. Roy Thomson Hall, the home of Toronto Symphony Orchestra, was a particularly great place to visit. I saw the ENT specialist for Canada Opera, who was very complimentary about my voice and said I had taken the correct course of action in cutting the set-list back.

That wasn't to be the only Canadian drama. As we arrived in Edmonton, I got pain in my left hip that was diagnosed as a trapped nerve. It was very painful and caused a heavy limp. I must have looked a right state, limping and coughing as I headed onto the Winspear Centre's stage! By the time we arrived in Vancouver in a blizzard, my body was finally starting to recover. I got my strength back and the dropped songs returned to the set-list. After further dates in Victoria Island and Calgary, we headed back into the United States. I particularly enjoyed singing at the Warners Theater in Los Angeles, which was a wonderful venue.

As the tour headed south, to Phoenix and on into Mexico, it was the equipment's turn to have difficulties. The heat meant we had technical problems as the antiquated sound desk struggled to cope. Mark Littlewood, who dealt with the front-of-house sound, found himself surrounded by several hundred very passionate Mexicans wanting his guts for garters. Mark came to me at the end of the show, telling me that many artists would have thrown the microphone down and walked away in such conditions. I told him I would never do that as it would be insulting his hard work, the promoter, and, most importantly, the audience who had paid money to see the show.

The next section of the tour was New Zealand, Australia, and Asia. After the intensity of the British and North American legs, I was pleased to find a bit more space between shows and to have a little bit of time to explore the areas we were visiting. We had a few days before our first show in Christchurch, so Julz and I and Jake, my tour manager, made our way to the beautiful city of Queenstown on South Island. This was bliss. Beautiful scenery, wonderful lake, great food, and lovely people—what's not to like? I thought to myself.

My guest artist on this part of the tour was a young, pretty Kiwi singer called Elizabeth Marvelly. Elizabeth is from Rotorua, and rightly proud of her Maori heritage. It's obvious in her performance of the Maori song "Tarakihi," which stirs people wherever in the world she performs it. Elizabeth and her parents were kind enough to show us round the area, famous for its volcanic activity. The activity is evidenced by the strong, unforgettable smell of sulphur.

After the New Zealand shows, including a performance in Auckland that I thought my best performance on tour to date, we flew on to Australia. Starting in Adelaide, I sang in Brisbane, Sydney, and Melbourne before heading on to Perth. When we got to Sydney, I took the opportunity to climb the famous Harbour Bridge. For safety, I used climbing clips to reach the amazing view at the top. It felt incredibly surreal that while I stood there with the opera house below me, the orchestra was down there rehearsing *my* show! Both Sydney Opera House and Hamer Hall in Melbourne were great venues to play. Both had stunning acoustics and, if anything, I thought Hamer Hall's acoustics were even better than those in Sydney.

Asia was another adventure, and the press conferences there were as crazy as my previous time in Hong Kong. In Seoul, there were so many camera flashes that I could feel the heat from them! The concerts in Seoul and Tokyo were similar in some ways but very different in others: the Korean audiences were less reserved than the Japanese, though the Japanese audiences always gave me a fantastic response at the end of every piece. Outside the cities, Julz and I particularly enjoyed our time in Busan in South Korea; it was sunny, warm, and very pretty, with a rugged coastline.

It was time for the final European leg, taking in Sweden, Norway, Denmark, Finland, and Holland. I was joined by Natasha Marsh for this part of the tour, and it was great to catch up with her again. The audiences across Europe were welcoming and enthusiastic, and the programme was back to a hectic five shows a week after the more restful pace in New Zealand, Australia, and Asia.

Whilst I was in Sweden, I got news that something extraordinary was happening in Germany. My initial audition on *Britain's Got Talent* was being used in an advert for Deutsche Telekom, and there had been a very strong reaction to it. The result was that *One Chance* was at number one in the German album charts, where it remained for seven weeks. My recording of "Nessun Dorma" reached number two in the singles charts in Germany on downloads alone.

I found myself going to Germany more and more. I was asked to perform at the opening of the German football league season, the Bundesliga at Bayern Munich's Allianz Arena. I went on an arena tour in Germany, Austria, and Switzerland, performing to audiences of over ten thousand people a night. It was more than I could ever have hoped for in any dream.

The craziest event I did was at the Dome in Mannheim. It was very much a youth event. I made my way onto the stage and was met with a wall of sound from teenage girls. When I told Julz, she didn't stop laughing for about fifteen minutes.

"You a pop star? Don't make me laugh!"

I found it bizarre, too. The noise was so loud that I couldn't hear myself or the backing track. I had to rely completely on memory and a little bit of luck to be in time and in tune. I was blown away by the fact that an operatic aria written nearly a hundred years before was causing such a reaction with a teenage audience. It proved to me what I had always known: that music can cross the boundaries of geography, age, class, and creed.

All in all, 2008 had been another incredible year. The travelling meant I hadn't seen much of my family and friends, but I stayed in touch as best as I could.

Julz and I had adapted to the pressures of both travelling round the world and spending time apart. Julz had also been a great interview partner who would lighten the mood with a deft comment about how daft her husband was.

I had feared doing fifty-five shows and truly believed I would crash and burn. I don't think I was the only one who thought that. But I learned an important lesson. Yes, there were obstacles. Yes, there were difficulties. But the only real obstacle in the end was in my own mind, and for the first time in my life I had overcome it. I performed more than a hundred live concerts that year—nearly double what I thought I could ever achieve.

CHAPTER FIFTEEN

On Reflection

WHEN IT WAS suggested that we do the photo shoot for my second studio album, *Passione*, in Venice, I readily agreed. Who wouldn't pass up the chance to spend time in one of the world's most beautiful cities? But come the day of the shoot I was regretting my enthusiasm; it was first thing on a crisp January morning, and although the city looked stunning, it was absolutely freezing. I was dressed in my tuxedo, when I could have done with my hat, scarf, and several more hours in bed.

I had started recording *Passione* in late 2008. Much of it was recorded in Stockholm, but also some in Prague. I wanted the record to have a more classical feel this time round, while remaining true to the audience that had bought my first album. Expectations were high, even though it is well known that for any artist it's rare for their second album to do better than the first.

I began by giving Simon Cowell and his team a playlist of

possible tracks, and then we worked together on selecting the material. Having sold more than three million albums of my debut, I now had more artistic control than when I'd recorded *One Chance*. However, I knew from experience that it was important to pick your battles carefully. Despite having spent eighteen months in the industry, I was still the one with the least experience. I knew it was important to listen to those with the expertise, while doing my best to create a record I was happy with.

During the selection process, we recorded demos of songs I loved and also some of the ones the A&R team thought would be good. That helped us make good progress. It's interesting how trying out a track in the studio can help decide whether a song is right or not. Sometimes the results can surprise you. I had found that with my version of the R.E.M. song "Everybody Hurts" on *One Chance*, and I would find it again here with an Italian version of the Procol Harum classic "A Whiter Shade of Pale."

On the other side of the coin, I tried one of my favourite Richard Marx songs, "Right Here Waiting," and it just didn't work. I was gutted because it is a great song, and one I felt would be good to have on the record. We ended up with a great playlist, including "La Prima Volta," the Italian version of Ewan McColl's "The First Time I Ever Saw Your Face," and "Un Giorno per Noi," a Nino Rota classic derived from his soundtrack to Franco Zeffirelli's *Romeo and Juliet*.

My only concern was that Simon wanted to have the full album in Italian. I was worried that this might make the album less approachable than the first. My management and I pushed to have at least a few songs in English, but Simon wasn't to be moved on it. Simon has always had the ability to read what the public wants to hear, so despite our misgivings we trusted his judgement. It was a subject that came up in interviews very frequently when on promotion. When asked why the whole album was recorded in Italian, I simply replied that it was a beautiful and very musical language to sing in.

The album being Italian, it made perfect sense for the photo shoot to take place in Venice. As I took my place in makeup, I decided to have a little fun. My manager, Vibica Auld, was with me on this trip, and swearing the makeup girls to secrecy, I gave her a quick ring.

"Hi, Vib," I said in my best just-got-out-of-bed voice, "I'm really sorry. I've overslept and only just woken up."

"Oh, Paul"—I could hear the worry in her voice—"the photo shoot's about to start. You should be down there and in makeup by now. I'll give them a ring and . . . "

She paused, as she could hear me laughing on the other end.

"You're winding me up, aren't you?" she replied.

"Been here all along," I confessed. "Don't forget your coat when you come down. It's absolutely perishing."

The release of the second album was different from the first. With *One Chance* there had been no real expectation of what might happen; now the anticipation was huge. This meant there was more pressure for the album to be successful, and a lot of promotional work had been lined up to achieve this.

I started the album promotion in my biggest market: Germany.

To my amazement, I was nominated for Germany's prestigious ECHO award—the German equivalent of the American Grammys or the Brit Awards in the UK. I was up for Best International Rock and Pop Artist and Album of the Year, finding myself against such established artists as Lenny Kravitz and Kid Rock.

With such stiff competition, I was convinced I was not going to win. Vivian Hauner from Sony, who had been working very hard to get me established in Germany, informed me that I would be performing "Nessun Dorma" at the awards ceremony, right before my category came up. This had me thinking, Are they telling me I'm going to win, or are they being malicious? Are they going to have me perform a piece about winning and then tell me I haven't won? That would certainly have been cruel!

It was another of those life-changing moments. I suspected that everyone but me knew whether I had won or not, and that they wanted my reactions to be genuine. I turned out to be right. Everyone from the German label knew the result, and this was clear when, to my amazement, my name was read out as the winner. I couldn't believe it!

As I continued promoting *Passione* round the world, the successes kept coming. With Julz at my side, we headed off to New Zealand and Australia, where I achieved a second number one in the former and a top-five album in the latter. Promotional tours can throw up some funny moments, and this was no exception. I was appearing on *Sunrise*, Australia's main weekday breakfast show, when the host asked if Julz was with me. Bearing in mind that it was not long after six in the morning and Julz hadn't been made up, honesty may not have been the best policy.

"Of course," I replied, "she's at the back of the studio."

The host's reaction was to call Julz to the set, where she stood behind me and made a motion to strangle me from behind. This got a great reaction both in the studio and from viewers at home, who sent her lots of messages of support.

From down under, we made our way to Canada and the United States. In New York, I was met by a film crew who wanted to show me round the city. I did an interview at the stunning Grand Central Terminal and while filming outside, was interrupted by a passing taxi driver.

"Hey, man!" he shouted out of his window. "I love your voice!"

New Yorkers have a formidable reputation for being hard to please, so it felt strange but amazing to be recognised in this way in such a big city.

I had to think on my feet during live interviews, and none more than on a local New York City TV station.

"It's a poignant moment for you to release an album around Mother's Day," the presenter said, "since your mum died a few years ago."

I was somewhat taken aback.

"Actually, when I spoke to my mum a few days ago," I corrected, "she was very much alive and well."

I had another early morning performance on the *Today* show, as well as appearances on *Good Morning America*, *Fox and Friends*, and *Oprah* again. It was an absolute honour to be invited back to perform on Oprah's show, especially as this was a show dedicated to her favourites. I performed a half-English, half-Italian version of "Memory."

Around this time, another *Britain's Got Talent* success story was starting back home. A middle-aged lady by the name of Susan Boyle had performed at the auditions in Glasgow and astounded the judges and the country with her rendition of "I Dreamed a Dream." I was asked about Susan in many interviews across the world as I went round promoting *Passione*. I was really happy that another person had been given the opportunity to change her life in the same way I had. *Britain's Got Talent* was proving to the world that it was giving people undreamed of opportunities. At the same time, I was aware that my show had taken place over a single week, whereas for Susan it would be over several weeks. I hoped she would cope with the pressure, and in an across-the-world interview, with me in Sydney and Susan in London for NBC in New York, I advised her to try and take it one day at a time.

After North America and more promotion across Europe, it was time for me to return to *Britain's Got Talent*. I had been asked to perform during one of the semi-final shows—my first time back on the show that had started it all for me. I was very aware of this, and when I was asked to rehearse my performance of "La Prima Volta" for the fifth time, my manager Vibica asked me whether I really wanted to. I preferred not to, as I feared giving my best performance in rehearsal, but at the same time I was desperate to perform well, so I went ahead.

Sure enough, I gave a really good rendition in this final rehearsal, which left me concerned I wouldn't be able to match it in the actual performance. When my time came to perform, nerves took over a little in the first half of the song; it took me half the song to fully get into it. I was bitterly disappointed in my performance, so it was great to hear Ant and Dec say, "Good ol' Pottsy!" after I'd finished.

The year continued apace. I went on a second world tour, which was pretty much as extensive as the first. Once again, there were many highlights: I performed in front of thirty-five thousand people in Seoul, and I don't think I'd ever seen so many people in one place; in Japan, I did a special performance of "Cavatina" for Julz, and read a surprise poem I'd written for her; I also headlined for the first time at the Royal Albert Hall.

As the end of the year approached, I was doing a Christmas tour in Norway and Sweden when I found myself going down with a heavy cold that was very close to laryngitis. Scandinavia is beautiful in the approach to Christmas, with an understated jingle of festivity. I couldn't enjoy it this time, however, as I had to stay wrapped up indoors because of the heavy cold. It couldn't have been worse timing, as my next performance, in Leipzig, was for the José Carreras Gala for Leukaemia Research.

I was desperate to perform for one of my childhood idols. I saw a doctor who gave me the once-over and banned me from flying, so we were forced to travel from Oslo to Leipzig by train. I kept myself going with good doses of hot water, lemon, and honey, and gave what I considered to be a reasonable performance of the wonderful operetta aria "Dein Ist Mein Ganzes Herz." I had a short chat with José after the performance; he told me that since he'd first heard me at the same event two years earlier,

I had made great progress and that I had a lovely instrument. I was honoured to get such a warm response.

Back home, decisions had been made about my future, and one of them was that my next album wouldn't be coming from Syco. There had been no fallout at all, just a mutual business decision. I kept in touch with the team at Syco, as they had become friends, not just colleagues. I was pleased that my management had faith in me and that even after leaving Syco, my singing career would go on.

I was excited about starting a new project where I would actually own the music I was producing. This brought independence and freedom, and with that of course came risk and responsibility. I had always planned that my next album would be based around music from the movies, so I spent some time in Scotland, walking through the beautiful landscape and immersed in soundtracks, looking for possible music to record. I interviewed potential producers to work with and made the decision to go with renowned film score producer Simon Franglen.

I chose the tracks carefully, and sung the languages based on how the music spoke to me. I still felt that the second album had been held back slightly by its sole use of Italian. Now it was my decision. I wanted to keep *Cinema Paradiso*, my third album, as approachable as possible. The tracks included pieces from *Breakfast at Tiffany's*, *Titanic*, and *The Godfather*. The most challenging track for me was Ryiuchi Sakamoto's "Forbidden Colours," which originally featured on the soundtrack to *Merry Christmas, Mr. Lawrence*. The accompaniment seemed to be deliberately working against me, and I made a few adjustments of my own to make it come together. It is now one of the favourite songs I have ever performed.

My third album wasn't to be my only link with the cinema. I had been approached by various people about the possibility of making a film based on my life story. These included Brad Weston and Mike Menchel, who had first spoken to me when they were at Paramount studios. As often happens with film projects, the movie had been mothballed and resurrected several times.

This time, though, things were different. I went over to Los Angeles and had a meeting with Brad, Mike, and Justin Zackham, who had written a screenplay. They had great news for me. Despite all the problems, they felt there was every chance the film would go ahead.

"It's a story that has to be told," they said to me, and it was difficult not to be inspired by their belief in the project.

Brad and Mike explained that they had found a renowned director to take the project on: David Frankel, who was responsible for movies like *Marley and Me* and *The Devil Wears Prada*. The number of Hollywood films that never get made is endless, but for the first time it really looked like the movie was going to happen.

I travelled the world again to promote *Cinema Paradiso*. On 31 December 2010, I performed at the Brandenburg Gate as part of Berlin's New Year celebrations. With fireworks going off behind me, I sang "Nessun Dorma" in front of a crowd of over a million people. It was such an honour to take part in a New Year event in such a great city. To perform in front of so many people meant that although the temperatures were at minus 12 degrees Celsius, I felt huge warmth.

* * *

Many countries I have performed in are close to my heart, but in early 2011 two of them in particular were struck by natural disasters. In February 2011, New Zealand was struck by a earthquake around the city of Christchurch. Then in March, an earthquake off the east coast of Japan triggered a deadly tsunami. I was startled by both events, and was moved to help.

I travelled at my own cost to Auckland to perform at a concert to raise money for the victims of the Christchurch earthquake. It was a long, long flight, and was almost in vain. I was put up in a gorgeous house by a man called Seaby, who had made his name in communications. Having the sea air by me, I left the ceiling-to-floor windows open all night. My foreign blood was obviously sweeter to the local mosquitoes, and I got eaten alive. By the eve of the concert, my left ankle was swollen and painful, forcing me to limp.

The next day the ankle was even worse and hot to the touch. I figured it was due to an allergic reaction, but Elizabeth Marvelly, who had organised the concert, took me to North Bay Hospital to get it checked out. It turned out to be cellulitis, which if left untreated can lead to septicaemia, and even be fatal. The doctor knew why I was in the country, and told me that ordinarily they would admit me for a few days to keep me under observation. She decided to make an exception, provided I took some powerful antibiotics and there were no adverse reactions.

The problem was, as I have said before, that I am a pincushion when it comes to needles. I'm not afraid of them, but my veins appear to be terrified and go away and hide. After an hour, it looked like I wasn't going to be able to perform. Then the hospital found someone from the intensive care unit who was used to working with patients with veins like mine. He struck gold, or rather blood. It turned out that this doctor was on his first day back at work after losing his mother in the earthquake. I dedicated "Nessun Dorma" to him that evening.

Following the New Zealand earthquake and tsunami in Japan, many foreign acts had cancelled their concerts—as many as 75 percent had decided not to travel. I was determined to go, however, if the local authorities said it was safe. Many fans were concerned, but I felt that to turn my back on people who had given me support for the last four years amounted to rejection. I felt very strongly that both New Zealand and Japan needed not only sympathy, but to have people start visiting there again, to bring in tourist dollars. I wanted to show a good example, so I travelled to Japan to perform as planned. I sang with the Yomiuri Symphony Orchestra in Tokyo, Yokohama, and Osaka; the orchestra was incredible, and I had the privilege of performing with them again in 2012.

While I was abroad again, this time on one of several tours of South Korea, shooting had started back in Europe on the film based on my life: *One Chance*. For all Brad's and Mike's confidence, I still couldn't quite believe it was actually happening. As part of his research for the film, I had taken director David Frankel round to some of the main sites of my life in Wales. We visited the church where Julz and I got married and the branch of Carphone Warehouse where I'd worked.

David also met our own version of Marley (of the film *Marley & Me*)—Caesar, who is every bit as incorrigible as Marley himself.

We got Caesar in December 2011. He was tiny, like a miniscule polar bear. Julz was desperate to get him as quickly as possible, so we drove over to Llangorse, close to Brecon, to pick him up. Even today, he is a big baby and often sings along to my performance of the *Godfather* theme. David immediately fell in love with Caesar, and Caesar loved him right back.

When the film locations were changed from Venice (for the Italian scenes) to the slightly less salubrious Port Talbot, I did my best to be available but unseen. There is nothing worse than to have someone observing you working all the time. I felt it best to leave James Corden, who had been chosen to play me, to get on with the job at hand.

Even so, I couldn't stay away completely. I was invited to the wedding scene, and it was incredibly strange to watch James and the fantastic Alexandra Roach walking down the aisle as me and Julz. Weirder still was the experience of watching one or two scenes I had recorded the vocals for a few weeks earlier. It was very strange indeed to see James's mouth open and shut and hear my own voice come out!

Inside the church, filming of the wedding scene had started and Julz and I were seated at the altar. I looked across to Julz and saw she was crying. David Frankel, whom I was sitting next to, also noticed.

"You know, she's crying! She's got really emotional about it."

I knew Julz better, however.

"Sorry, David, but those are tears of laughter!"

I could see why. To us both, the whole thing was surreal. We were Julz and Paul, and yet standing in front of us were some of the biggest stars of stage and screen playing us. My life had thrown up many strange moments over the previous few years, but this was one of the most bizarre.

Many people describe their lives as a roller-coaster ride, but mine feels as though it has had more ups and downs than most. There were certainly plenty of downs to begin with: struggling around other people and finding myself the communal punch-bag left me feeling so low and pointless that when a predatory sex offender took me under his "wing" I did nothing to stop him. I was an easy target.

Singing was the only genuine escape I had. I found myself fighting to keep it just mine, and then discovered that in order to keep doing it, I would actually need to share it with others. This was not an easy thing to do: to open up my singing to others also meant opening it up to scrutiny, and for others to say it was not good enough.

The world has become more aware of bullying and abuse, but that doesn't necessarily mean that it deals with it better, or that it is easier for the victims of bullying and abuse to deal with it. It remains as much a challenge as ever. Ignoring it doesn't make it go away; that much hasn't changed. The biggest challenge for those it affects is to be able to remain objective about what is happening and not take it personally. How do you ignore the bullies without bottling up how it makes you feel? I still don't know how to do this.

I am in a much better place than I was then, but for someone with my experience it's still not easy to accept the good things that happen. I will always wonder whether I am good enough, or whether I deserve the success I have enjoyed during the last six years or so. This drives a sense of insecurity that will never leave me.

Some insecurity can be very helpful in keeping your feet on the ground and pushing you on to improve. My confidence has indeed grown, and my shyness is much less obvious, but it is still there when I meet someone new, or find myself in a crowded situation. Crowds are still difficult for me, and I have to put myself into "public" mode to fight against the desire to go and hide in a corner. This will sometimes lead me to talk too much, to try and justify myself, or to bury myself in my phone and pretend the world around me isn't there.

With everything I have been through, I have learned a number of lessons along the way. It is so important to be true to yourself. When a drastic change happens to you in the way it did to me in 2007, it's easy to be caught up in the excitement of what's happening. Lots of people will tell you how fantastic you are, and the most dangerous thing to do is to believe them.

Britain's Got Talent saved me from myself. It meant that I was no longer a person defined by the difficult times I had been through. Those things still exist, but I have proved to myself, and hopefully to others, that I *can* get past obstacles if only I believe in myself a little more.

I will always be incredibly grateful to *Britain's Got Talent* and Syco for giving me the opportunities I've had. But the fact that I'm still performing round the world six years later is about more than just the programme. It is thanks to many things: to my management team at Modest! for their belief in me; to the record labels that have supported me; to Simon Cowell, Amanda Holden, and Piers Morgan for giving me that first opportunity; and if I allow myself a little credit, it's also down to hard work. While it is definitely better than a proper job, you can't have back what you don't put in, let alone get interest on top!

There are other people who have been instrumental in my success, too. Julz has been my rock and my steadying hand throughout the twelve years we've been together and the ten years we've been married. It's been fantastic to have the support of both mine and Julz's family throughout. We've all found it very bewildering at times, but incredible all the time. None of this would still be happening if it weren't for the support of people round the world who have bought my albums.

I would like to thank all those who have made me feel at home in their countries. There have been so many wonderful places I've been fortunate enough to visit that there isn't the space to list them all here. But no matter where I travel, there is only one place I can call home: the United Kingdom and, in particular, Port Talbot. It is my adopted home, of course, but I have always been made to feel welcome here. That is why Julz and I have stayed. You can live in the largest mansion, but if it doesn't feel like home, then it isn't home.

I found my voice and my voice found me. Without it, I don't know where I would be. One of the most random decisions of my life took me to Dreamland.

Life doesn't come with a sat nav. You will often hear directions and advice, but they won't always be helpful. Sometimes the only way to go the right way is to learn the hard lessons of going the wrong way. Yes, there may be twists and turns along the way, but if you have the determination and belief to keep going, then anything is possible. So the next time you're looking in the mirror and thinking, I can't do it—challenge yourself. You never know what you're capable of until you give it the best shot you can.

Thank you for walking beside me over the last six years.

ACKNOWLEDGMENTS

A S A NON-PROFESSIONAL WRITER I'd like to thank my editor, Tom Bromley, for his support and guiding hand. It has been a rewarding challenge, and with Tom's support it has been made enjoyable. I'd also like to thank Amanda Murray at Weinstein Books and Leslie Wells for their further guidance. Finally, I'd like to thank Vibica Auld for being there to (metaphorically, of course) crack the whip to keep me on target.